5-MINUTE
BIBLE STUDIES
for
TEENS

Clark Schultz

NORTHWESTERN PUBLISHING HOUSE
Milwaukee, Wisconsin

Northwestern Publishing House
N16W23379 Stone Ridge Drive, Waukesha WI 53188-1108
www.nph.net
© 2019 Northwestern Publishing House
Published 2019
Printed in the United States of America
ISBN 978-0-8100-3022-0
ISBN 978-0-8100-3023-7 (e-book)

21 22 23 24 25 26 27 28   10 9 8 7 6 5 4 3

PREFACE

In 2011, a popular comic book company did something remarkable and, for their purposes, marketable. They reinvented all of their old classic comic book heroes. They reimagined the heroes' origin stories and gave the reader a new look at each character. They called this relaunch of comics "The New 52." When asked to do this Bible study project, I wanted to take a cue from that comic book company. Obviously, I am not changing the pages of God's infallible Word. My thought was to take some of my favorite biblical characters and stories and draw them into a 21st-century spotlight.

My prayer is that over "The Next 52" weeks, as you read each short devotion, the Spirit will move you to put yourself in the shoes, or sandals, of these original biblical heroes to see how their lives can still teach lessons. The main lesson is, of course, to look to Christ as our ultimate hero!

For my family, my brothers, and the teens

Adam—Fearfully and Wonderfully Made

❖

Then God said, "Let us make mankind in our image, in our likeness, so that they may rule over . . . all the creatures that move along the ground." GENESIS 1:26

Context: Genesis 1:26,27; 2:5-7

I love the smell of something new, whether it's a car, the latest cell phone, or an appliance. The excitement of opening the box, tearing off the protective coating, and playing with the product brings a smile to my face even as an adult.

When God created humans, did our Creator have that same feeling? He took a clump of dirt and formed the eyes, the ears, and the spleen (I mean, come on, who doesn't need a spleen?). What joy God must have had as he looked at this special creature, made *in his own image!* Scripture even says that at the end of each day, God observed, "It is good."

How awesome for Adam to be able to take care of the new world. To show perfect love to his spouse, his job, and, most important, his God.

Due to sin, life loses that new car smell, and life, for lack of a better word, stinks. Fortunately for us, we have a Savior who covers the stench of our sin with more than just a deodorizer. He covers us with his blood, so when God sees us, it's like the first time he looked at a perfect Adam and Eve. Ah, that smells and sounds good!

- What gets in the way of our having that "new" or "fearfully and wonderfully made" (Psalm 139:14) feeling?

- Think of someone right now who could use a good word from you to make their day!

Pray: Lord, thank you for creating me and thank you for your Son, who has made me new!

The Devil Strikes Back

❖

Now the serpent was more crafty than any of the wild animals the LORD God had made. He said to the woman, "Did God really say . . . ?" GENESIS 3:1

Context: Genesis 3:1-7

What was I thinking?

How many times have those words crossed our lips and minds? The time I knew I shouldn't go to that party, and now I'm suspended from the team. The time I knew I shouldn't send that angry text, and now I've lost a friend. The list could go on and on—and, sadly, it does.

The moment Adam and Eve took their first bites of forbidden fruit, sin filled their veins. Perfection was lost forever. Since then, sinners like you and me have been asking this question: *What was I thinking?* The devil works overtime on us, using the same tactics he used on our first parents. As he did with them, he gets us to doubt God and to mistrust his promises or, worse, to think God is keeping something good from us. So when bad things happen, we end up questioning God's love.

God doesn't love us? Friends, nothing could be further from the truth. God could have been done with Adam and Eve and tossed them away like trash, but instead he gave them a promise. He promised a Savior who took our every *what was I thinking* moment to the cross with him and forgives us. Smile, and think more about what God is thinking!

- What *what was I thinking* moment weighs heavily on your heart?

- Where specifically in your daily battle does Satan act like a military strategist and attack you at your weak points?

- In Christ, what does God think about you?

Pray: Heavenly Father, thank you for not giving up on me, even though many times I have said or done things I regret.

A New Hope

❖

"He will crush your head, and you will strike his heel."
GENESIS 3:15
Context: Genesis 3:8-15

The people in the crowd waved to their heroes. History had been made, and now the admirers stood ten deep on the confetti-filled streets, trying to get a glimpse of those heroes. Several generations of family members had waited for this day to come. After many years, the supposed curse had been broken and the team was victorious. There were smiles and high fives among perfect strangers. There was an optimism that had not been felt in this city for over a century. Chicago had won the World Series.

Quite a few centuries earlier, our world was plunged into sin. Since that game changer, we have been living under the curse of the law. And we can't escape the facts: "The wages of sin is death" (Romans 6:23). To punch our ticket to the big game, we have to keep all of God's law perfectly. But we whiff and strike out every day. We sin! Like our first parents, we would rather finger-point or blame God than admit guilt. In response, God sent his Son in relief to finish the game for us. He took the blows the devil threw at him. And though at times the devil seemed victorious, Jesus made history by crushing the head of the serpent. We now have a VIP pass to the front of the line of God's forgiveness. We win! High-five the next person you meet. Because of Jesus, they are winners too!

- What prevents us from living like winners?

- How do you define hope?

- Where does our hope come from?

Pray: Jesus, when life feels like I'm going into extra innings with no strength left, remind me to look to you alone for relief.

Boys Will Be Boys, Part 1

❖

Abel kept flocks, and Cain worked the soil.
GENESIS 4:2

Context: Genesis 4:1–4a

As a father of three boys, I notice their differences—especially between the older two. One likes wheels and tractors, while the other likes balls. One is so terrified of water that he cried the entire time we were at a water park, even while on the tame ride down the aptly named "lazy" river. However, the other son is ready to dive into the bathtub, or any other receptacles in our bathroom that hold water. They came from the same parents but have totally different personalities.

The same can be said of the two sons in our reading for today. Cain was a farmer and tilled the earth. Abel was a shepherd and looked after the sheep. Both worked in different areas with the differing gifts that God gave them. Their personalities in gift giving were quite different as well.

Where do you find yourself working in God's creation? Are you the leading older child, keeping your siblings in line? Are you the well-adjusted middle child? Are you an only child? Or are you, like me, the baby of the family who can do no wrong? Wherever you are in your family's birth order, rejoice that God has made you his redeemed child through Christ. Beyond that, he has made you as you are. He has given you different gifts to serve him. Life is too short to compare yourself to others. Be the you that God made you to be!

- How does the following quote apply to the gifts God has given you: "Everyone else is taken, so be you"?

- How does the knowledge that God has redeemed you through Christ influence what you do with your life?

Pray: Lord, use me today, along with the gifts you have given me, to make a difference in your creation.

4

Boys Will Be Boys, Part 2

❖

"If you do not do what is right, sin is crouching at your door."
GENESIS 4:7

Context: Genesis 4:4b–12

What is the first sin you remember committing? When I was five years old, my brother took me to the local fireman's picnic. He told me to grab all of the prizes on the table by the carnival games. Being an obedient brother, I walked up to the carnival worker, smiled, grabbed as many trinkets as I could squeeze into my chubby little hands, and ran. Needless to say, I got caught, was forced to return the items—with an apology—and was sent to my room.

That was not my first sin, and it certainly wouldn't be my last. And you are in the same place I am. We may have made poor choices in relationships, backstabbed our friends, cheated on tests, and more. Sometimes these sins have led to other sins. Cain did not wake up one day and decide to kill his brother. Instead, he let his sins of jealousy and hatred fester. This led to the first murder recorded in human history. It was not among two warring clans but among two brothers who had shared a home and a supper table.

The devil works overtime on us. The sin may start small but then fester and grow until one day we look in the mirror and ask, *How did I get here?* Fortunately, we have our big brother, Jesus, who went to the cross for us. He paid for all our sins—those that have resided in the sin circus in our brains and those that we've acted out. Knowing that Jesus forgives our every sin is the one thing that brightens our day.

- What sin is crouching at your door?

Pray: Lord, give me the strength to let go of past hurt and guilt and to find comfort in your healing forgiveness.

The Lord Will Be the Lord

❖

Then the LORD said to Cain, . . .
GENESIS 4:9

Context: Genesis 4

When I was in college, I saw a movie in which the immature main character wanted to impress his girlfriend by adopting a child. Needless to say, the pseudo father figure knew nothing about raising a child. He let this five-year-old eat whatever he wanted and do whatever he pleased. In one memorable scene, this young boy was taught that when he had "an accident," instead of cleaning up the mess, this "big daddy" would put newspaper on the floor to cover it up.

Though we may chuckle, we know we do the same thing in real life. When confronted with a sin, we sweep it under the table and pretend it didn't happen. When God confronted Cain, he, like his parents, tried to pass the blame. But what did God do?

As you read Genesis chapter 4, count the number of times you see the words "the LORD." While this name has lost some of its luster over time, the Israelites recognized it as a clear reference to the God of promise. In a world where people make and break promises, this is refreshing to hear and read. God sought out Adam and Eve, he sought out their wayward son, and he seeks us out. He wants to remind us daily not to cover or hide our sins but to take them to him because he forgives us. He promises!

- What does the fact that God keeps all of his promises mean for you?

Pray: Lord, by nature I want to cover my sin, but I realize I cannot. Help me to see that only through your blood is the multitude of my sins covered.

Babblers

❖

Now the whole world had one language.

GENESIS 11:1

Context: Genesis 11:1-9

I jokingly say that if I could build a time machine, there are two places and times I would go to. The first journey would take me back so that I could stop the writer of the first mathematical word problem—those mind bending questions like: *Two trains are driving toward each other. The first train leaves Town A at 5 A.M. traveling 60 miles per hour. The second train leaves Town B at 7 A.M. traveling 70 miles per hour. The distance between Town A and Town B is 455 miles. What is the EXACT time that the collision will occur?* I once responded to my teacher with "x = who cares." That wasn't one of my better moments. The second place I would travel back in time to visit would be the Tower of Babel. Once there, I would boldly say, "Hey, Babel people. Put the bricks down. It is because of you that I am failing Spanish."

Read Genesis 11:1-9. "One language"? Wow! How easy that would have been! But with ease came complacency, and with complacency came the need to think they knew more than God. Sound familiar? Yes, when life is going great, we tend to focus more on our own world. But God wants us to focus on him and on ways we can serve him and others.

As always, our motivation for doing this is not this five-minute devotion but rather our triune God—the Father who created us, the Son who redeemed us, and the Spirit who equips us.

- In what areas of life do you tend to be more complacent?

Pray: Lord, help me to think less about ways to please myself and more about ways to serve you and my neighbor.

WEEK 3 DAY 2

Triune God

❖

The LORD came down to see . . .
GENESIS 11:5

Context: Genesis 11:5-7

In George Orwell's novel *1984,* you are introduced to "Big Brother," the leader of a society in which every citizen is under constant surveillance by the authorities. In modern culture, the phrase "Big Brother" has entered the mainstream as a synonym for abuse of power, particularly in respect to civil liberties and often specifically related to mass surveillance. The idea of hidden cameras, tapped phone lines, and 24-hour surveillance can be frightening.

Big Brother IS watching you. Before you call your local police, rest easy, because this is nothing to be creeped out about. Instead, God sees and knows everything. God knew what was happening with the people at Babel. God knew what was in their hearts and wanted to put a stop to their rebellion. God sees us and knows us. Yes, it may be quite alarming to know that God was there on our last date. God was there when we sent that last text or the chat that we quickly deleted. But, like the people at Babel, God will save us from ourselves. His judgment to scatter the people prevented their sin of pride from destroying them.

God may bring a pastor, a friend, a parent, or a teammate into our lives who will steer us from going down a road that would lead us from him. Or he may allow something to happen that will prevent even greater damage to our faith. Rest easy. God is watching. He knows what is best for each of us. That is comforting.

- Whom has God put into your life to help steer you closer to him and his Word?

Pray: Lord, thank you for keeping an eye on me. Please keep looking out for me.

Scatterers

❖

From there the Lord scattered them over the face of the whole earth. GENESIS 11:9

Context: Genesis 11:5-9

To help me the first time I was going to do laundry away from home, my mother had written instructions on a 3 x 5 note card: "Put the whites in with the whites, and put the colored clothes in with the colored clothes." Simple instructions. But like many simple things, they are simply forgotten. I knew better, but I needed to save time, so guess what? That white dress shirt is covered with pink, blue, and green spots. If I had just listened, I would have saved a little bit of money and a great deal of embarrassment.

The people at the Tower of Babel learned a similar lesson, only with much more serious results. God had told them to spread out and fill the whole earth. Their response? Thanks, but no thanks, God; we know better. In the end, God accomplished what he wanted to accomplish. He wanted the people to spread out, and spread out they did. But before we throw a brick at them, let's evaluate our own spiritual walk with God. God has given us his commandments to follow. But sometimes we feel that we know better. Like a hurried student who ignores his mother's advice as he loads the laundry, we mix our own thoughts together with the world's corrupt views and somehow expect that everything will come out clean. Our guilty consciences and damaged relationships show how foolish we are. Thankfully, Jesus came to be our very own spot remover. He washed us clean in his blood and gives us a fresh chance every day. Ironically, he uses words, his Word, to communicate that important message to us.

- In what ways can the diversity of languages be considered both a blessing and a challenge?

- God isn't necessarily calling you to spread out into the world. But what is God calling you to do today?

Pray: Lord, lead me to trust in you above all things, even if I think my way seems better. Your ways and will are always best.

Noah—The Builder

❖

Noah did everything just as God commanded him.

GENESIS 6:22

Context: Genesis 6:14-22

While in college, my classmates and I would look for crazy ways to entertain ourselves. One night, we decided to grab food trays from the cafeteria and go sledding down the hill behind our dorm. It was a blast!

Your turn: What is something you remember doing that was a bit "out there"?

The guy in our text did something crazy. He built a boat that was bigger than a football stadium. But that's not the crazy part. He built the boat on dry land, away from the water. Why did he build such a boat? Because God commanded him to do so. Noah took the jabs from his fellow people who thought he had lost his marbles. Sadly, those people found out what loss was as they lost their lives in the flood. Only Noah and his family were saved, because they listened to the voice of God.

People in today's world look at us like we are crazy because we believe in things like a six-day creation and God's perfect plan for marriage. No one reading this is perfect; we all can drudge up crazy stories that have less to do with innocent fun and more to do with sin. Fortunately, the confidence we have is not found in ourselves but in Christ, who did the craziest thing for you and me. He kept the law perfectly in our place and then took the punishment for our sin upon himself. Sometimes it may seem like you are sledding down a hill of despair or paddling a boat in the middle of a desert. Always remember that because of Jesus, God is with you all the way.

- What similarities do you see between Noah's situation and your own?

Pray: Lord, help me to trust your voice and your promises even when the world calls me crazy.

Noah—The Drinker

❖

When he drank some of its wine, he became drunk.

GENESIS 9:21

Context: Genesis 9:20-23

They say that loose lips sink ships. How about this one: "Too many sips can make you look like an idiot"? In the world of bars and taverns, there is a tradition of having 21 shots on one's 21st birthday. (Whatever happened to the practice of getting a free piece of dessert?) Aside from being extremely dangerous, attempting this tradition has made many look foolish and has caused many to sin.

Some of my most embarrassing moments came from having a sip too many. Noah was no different. He let one turn to two and then to three, and before long he was lying naked in front of his kids. When used in moderation and in line with the law of the state, the use of alcohol is not wrong. Drinking alcohol is not condemned in the Bible. However, the Bible clearly speaks against taking it to excess.

Fortunately, Noah had two sons who did not want their father to be disgraced. Shem and Japheth had their father's back—they covered him up. They knew he had messed up, and they didn't want to bring any further shame to their father. God knows we mess up. He wants us to run to him and his Son and know that his Son's blood covers our multitude of sins.

- What friend or family member has your back spiritually?

- Whose back do you have as a true friend?

Pray: God, forgive me for the times I have gotten myself under the influence of what the world says is cool. Please surround me with friends who will look out for my best interests, and make me into the kind of friend who will look out for theirs.

WEEK 4 DAY 3

Noah Lives Somewhere Under God's Rainbow

❖

"I have set my rainbow in the clouds, and it will be the sign of the covenant between me and the earth."
GENESIS 9:13

Context: Genesis 9:12-17

The munchkins sing, and the green witch tries snatching the red slippers. The desire for a brain, courage, and a heart. And oh . . . those flying monkeys. Man, they still give me nightmares. And, to top it all off, you have a song about a rainbow. *The Wizard of Oz*—what a classic! Black and white in one scene to a spectacular explosion of fruity colors in the next.

What stories Noah must have told around the campfire. He spent over a year in the ark, feeding and taking care of all the smelly animals and wondering when he would ever see dry ground. If you were Noah, what would you have done the minute you got off the ark? I would have kissed the ground and done a cartwheel. (And what a sight my 200-pound cartwheel would have been.)

But what made all the difference in the world was the rainbow. What a sight for Noah to behold! It was God's promise that he would never send another flood to destroy the whole world. God reminds us of that promise every time we see a rainbow. Yes, life sometimes seems pretty black and white—every day bringing the winter blahs or the ho hum of monotony. However, God's rainbow reminds us of the beauty of the plan he has for us and that he will make things work out for us. He has more than a pot of gold waiting for us; he has heaven! Hang on, it's more than somewhere over there. . . . It is a reality.

- We hear promises every day. What is different about God's promises?

Pray: Lord, help me to see through the raindrops of life to recognize the beauty of your plans for me.

Abram Leaves His Comfort Zone

❖

The LORD had said to Abram, "Go from your country, your people and your father's household to the land I will show you." GENESIS 12:1

Context: Genesis 11:27–12:1

To save ourselves from the boredom of dorm life in college, we would sometimes dream up spontaneous games. Or we would jump into a car and drive. Where? We would know when we got there. It could be a few towns over for half-price appetizers. Or wherever. Now, as adults, we feel the pressure of always having to know where we are going. We have the help of a GPS and online maps to give us the most direct route to where we need to go. Technology, while a blessing, takes the thrill out of new adventures to be had on the open road.

What a rush Abram must have had when God took him out of his comfort zone and called him to a distant land. Can you imagine the conversation?

"Hey, Abram."

"Yes, God?"

"I want you to go on a journey."

"Okay. Where to, God?"

"I will tell you when you get there."

How does one pack for that? Would you have gone? Abram did, and his life was never the same. God had great plans for him.

God has great plans for you too. God invites you to go on this adventure we call life with him in the lead. Abram's faith led him from Ur to the ride of a lifetime with God. May God bless you as you move on to the next adventure life brings your way.

• Where is God calling you?

Pray: Lord, lead me to step out of my comfort zone, knowing you are with me every step of the way.

WEEK 5 DAY 2

A Trusting Choice

❖

Lot chose for himself the whole plain of the Jordan.
GENESIS 13:11
Context: Genesis 13:5-13

There is a strategy to follow when eating pizza with a friend. As soon as the pizza is plopped down between the two of you, the game begins. You both study, analyze, and do a higher form of geometry to figure out which pieces are the biggest. The smart and gracious friend-move would be to let your friend go first and pray that he or she takes a smaller piece.

In our reading, Abram took the high road and allowed his nephew, Lot, to pick first whatever land he wanted for himself. Abram knew God had blessed him and would continue to bless him no matter what land he ended up with. Lot, on the other hand, saw the well-watered land—the Jordan plain—staring him in the face and took the best. He did the math in his head and concluded that the influence of the heathen people living there was a risk he was willing to take for a great piece of real estate. His eyes for the world took his focus away from the only thing that mattered: God.

In the world of advertising, you are told you need more, bigger, and supersized. Abram trusted God to give him what he needed and, as a result, was blessed ten times over. In his Word, God reminds us that he will provide for us daily. We can relax. With Jesus, we will always have the best piece of real estate: a place in heaven.

- When faced with decisions, where do we put our focus and trust?

- How can you be a gracious friend today?

Pray: When I'm faced with choices, Lord, help me to look to you for guidance, trusting that you will bless my decisions.

14

WEEK 5 DAY 3

Abram's Shield

❖

"Do not be afraid, Abram. I am your shield."
GENESIS 15:1

Context: Genesis 15:1-6

Many comic book heroes have costume features that make them stand out, such as an iron suit, a cape, or a mask. One hero in particular carries a shield made of the strongest metal known on earth: Vibranium. Of course, this metal does not exist on the real periodic table but was invented in the mind of a comic book writer. This mythical metal is impenetrable and protects our hero in any kind of battle.

Each day we put on costumes for work or school. They may not be as flashy as a red cape or as eye-catching as a quiver of arrows. However, there is something we put on that protects us more than any fictitious metal. It is the armor of God. By faith, Christ clothes us with his breastplate of righteousness and his belt of truth.

In the comic book story, the hero faces a bad guy who tried to cause trouble. We also have our enemies who try to turn us off course and to lead us into spiritual danger. And, some days, it seems like those enemies are winning. But Abram learned firsthand what it means to be under the protection of a true hero. That hero isn't found on the big screen. He's our big and almighty God. He is with us, and he is our shield, just as he was Abram's shield. Stand behind his shield and trust that no matter what comes your way, you do not need to be afraid.

- What are you afraid of?

- How do the heroes of the comics compare to our God?

Pray: Lord, even if I don't understand why things happen, help me to look to you as my shield and to know you will work all things out for my good.

Abraham Prays Boldly

❖

Then Abraham spoke up again: "Now that I have been so bold as to speak to the Lord, . . ."
GENESIS 18:27

Context: Genesis 18:1-33

The first time you ask your parents if you can borrow the keys to the car can be a trying experience. I wanted to go to the movies, so I did what any mature teenager would do. First, I asked my mom for permission. She gave the classic Mom response, "Go ask your father." So with sweaty palms and a heartbeat that resembled a jumping bean, I went to my dad and asked for the keys to the car. His response? "Yes."

Abraham knew that God had plans to destroy Sodom and Gomorrah, but he also knew that God is a loving and gracious God. So he dared to make a request of God. Luther reminds us that when we pray to God, "We may pray to him as boldly and confidently as dear children ask their dear father." Now, in the end, God did not answer Abraham's prayer exactly the way Abraham wanted. Sodom was destroyed. But he did spare Lot from the destruction.

God can answer our prayers in three ways: *no, yes,* and *wait.* And sometimes the answer is no because he has something better in mind. What is weighing on your mind? Go to God. He is listening, and he wants you to talk to him. Take comfort in the fact that he has more to give than the keys to an old beater car. He gives us the keys to heaven.

- What is the first prayer you remember learning?

- How has your prayer life changed from when you were young?

Pray: Give me boldness to talk to you, God, and confidence in whatever answer you give.

A Lot of Issues

❖

"Look, I have two daughters. . . ." GENESIS 19:8
Context: Genesis 19:8

In a recent *Wall Street Journal* article, Texas Republican Joe Barton was quoted as saying that child pornography is approaching a 20-billion-dollar-a-year business. Pornography used to be limited to magazines, but now it is just a click away. This oftentimes hidden sin can infect young and old, Christian and non-Christian alike. Our society greatly influences how we view sexual sins such as this. In our lesson, Lot was being confronted by the men of Sodom who wanted to have sex with the angels whom God had sent to save Lot. Lot's answer to their plea shows his senses had become dulled to the surroundings and the sexual sins that infested his hometown. His plan? "Instead of raping the men, take my two daughters and rape them."

Excusing a sin by committing another sin is wrong. Our mind can always rationalize, "It's just a picture or a video. It's not like I am acting on any of these impulses." Wrong! Stop listening to the world and listen to the voice of your God who loves you. Though the sin of pornography dishonors God by violating a very special gift he gave us, it is also very much forgiven in the cross of Christ. He paid for every glance, every turn of the page, and every click of the button.

Lot needed help getting out of the city that was swallowing his faith. God provides help for you in his Word, through your pastor, or through a Christian counselor. This assistance is also just one click away.

- How does society influence your idea of what sin is?

- If you are struggling with pornography or know someone who is, what steps can you take to help overcome the addiction?

Pray: Jesus, I need your help and strength to battle the temptations of the world around me.

A Lot More Issues

❖

He hesitated, . . . but Lot's wife looked back.
GENESIS 19:16,26

Context: Genesis 19:15-26

Over 1,500 people died the night the RMS *Titanic* sank, including passengers and crew. One of the first lifeboats to leave the *Titanic* carried only 28 people; it could have held 65. There were enough life jackets for all 2,208 people, and most everyone was wearing one.

But perhaps because they believed the ship was unsinkable, the lifeboat drills had been cancelled and the crew members weren't sure how many people the lifeboats could safely hold. It was also reported that when the warning was given that the ship was sinking, some laughed and continued partying, refusing to take the warning seriously.

Lot received the warning that God was going to torch his hometown. You would not have to warn me twice. Yet the Bible says Lot hesitated. And later when the town was being destroyed, Lot's wife looked back. Why? They had grown accustomed to the lifestyle and the world around them. They could not let go of it. If God came knocking today, could we part with the big screens, smartphones, and stuff we just have to have? It is not wrong to have nice things, but when these things overshadow the First Commandment and supersede God in our hearts, then, like Lot, we need to let them go and let God be our top priority. With him, we won't sink.

- What in this life makes you hesitate and keeps you from going all-in with God?

Pray: Lord, help me to let go of all the things of this world and give me the strength not to look back at them but to look to you alone as my number-one priority.

Abraham—The Wait Is Over

❖

**Sarah became pregnant and bore a son
to Abraham in his old age.**
GENESIS 21:2
Context: Genesis 21:1–5

What is the longest you have had to wait for something? For me, the wait was for the next movie in a series. I remember watching a scene where the hero of the story was frozen in carbonite and stolen away in a bounty hunter's ship. Shortly after that, his friends blasted off into space in search of him . . . and the movie ended. As the closing credits came rolling across the screen, I turned to my fifth grade teacher, who had taken a few die-hard fans to the movie, and asked, "When is the next movie coming out?" He said, "In another three years." To a nine-year-old, those three years might as well have been a million.

Abraham waited 25 years for the fulfillment of God's promise to him of a son. During that time, Abraham had his ups and downs, but he held on to his promise from God. He knew that, despite the way things seemed at times, God always kept his promises. And now he was finally holding the fulfillment of that promise in his hands.

Sometimes God's answer to our prayers may be to wait. He does not do this to play with us but to teach us to trust him. He sees the big picture; we do not. He will grant us what we need in his perfect time. He promised a Savior to Adam and Eve. Many died waiting for that promise, but God still kept it. If God can keep a great promise like that, you can be assured that he will certainly keep every other promise he makes.

- What are the benefits of waiting?

Pray: Lord, remind me to trust you in all things, even when I must wait.

19

Abraham Passes the Test

❖

**Then God said, "Take your son, your only son,
whom you love—Isaac—and go to the region of Moriah.
Sacrifice him there as a burnt offering
on a mountain I will show you."**
GENESIS 22:2

Context: Genesis 22:1-14

What is the hardest test you have ever taken? Was it your driver's test? A semester final? Or maybe, if you are like me, it was the ACT test I took . . . three times. The purpose of tests is to see what we know. They also serve as a learning tool.

Abraham waited 25 years for the promise of his son to be fulfilled. Then, when the boy was still young, God told Abraham to sacrifice Isaac. This may seem perplexing. However, consider two things. First, God wanted to see whom Abraham loved more: Isaac or the God who blessed him with his son. Second, we see that Abraham trusted God to keep his promises. God had said that through Isaac the promise of a Savior would come. Abraham knew that no matter what, God does not lie and he does not break promises.

When God allows tests and trials to come into our lives, it isn't to punish us but to bring us closer to him or to teach us. Sometimes these tests help us realize what is more important in our lives: God or whatever else threatens to take his place in our hearts. In any case, God is never intending to punish us. Jesus took our punishment. God always has our best interests in mind.

- What trials or tests are you currently struggling with?

Pray: Lord, remind me that no matter what I am facing, you are bigger and can help me through every trial or test.

WEEK 7 DAY 3

Isaac Gets a Wife

❖

She took her veil and covered herself.
GENESIS 24:65

Context: Genesis 24:1-67

Stores really know how to pour on the pressure during the holidays: if you really love your significant other, you will naturally want to spend the money to buy them something precious. Sometimes people buy into the thinking that the higher the price tag, the more precious the gift.

Do you have someone precious in your life? Or does God still have you waiting for Mr. or Miss Right? In either case, what do you look for in a relationship? Looks? Compatibility? Money? The skyrocketing divorce rate in our society gives us a reason to stop and think. And where does faith fit into the equation?

The answer may seem simple: Keep God number one in your relationship. A seminary professor once shocked our class by beginning his lecture this way: "Gentlemen, my wife loves someone else more than she loves me." There was shocked silence and maybe some deer-in-the-headlight looks from us; we were uncomfortable that he was sharing such an intensely personal and private topic. He then went on to say, "My wife loves Jesus more than me, and because of that, I will never be second." His point, of course, was that when looking for love, we should keep God as the main focal point. Looks and bank accounts can fade and disappear, but the love of Christ lasts forever. That is why Abraham was so adamant that Isaac not take a wife from the heathen people who lived nearby. What's way cool is that Isaac accepted the wife his father's servant chose without even seeing her face, because he knew her true beauty lay within her faith!

- What qualities do you look for in a boyfriend or girlfriend?

Pray: Jesus, when I am ready to find my spouse, help me to find someone who loves you more than anything in this world. If you have blessed me with this someone, I say THANK YOU!

It's Better to Receive Than Deceive

❖

"Your brother came deceitfully and took your blessing."
GENESIS 27:35
Context: Genesis 27:1-35

For decades, most comedy shows followed a common theme. Pick any one at random and you will probably see this story play out: Someone tells a white lie. Then, throughout the whole show, the lie escalates to a catastrophic conclusion. Finally, the actors have their moment of enlightenment: "Had I just told the truth, none of this mess would have happened."

It doesn't take a rocket scientist to realize that we all tell lies. It's in our DNA. We lie to our teachers about why our homework is not done. We lie to our parents about why we missed curfew AGAIN. We deceive ourselves when we imagine that God does not know. When we lie, we step into Satan's trap of thinking it is better to look innocent than to be innocent.

Jacob lied to his father. This caused his brother, Esau, to hate him so much that Jacob was forced to leave home. Isaac and Rebekah, their parents, were not innocent. Isaac knew that God wanted Jacob to be blessed, but Isaac wanted the blessing to go to Esau. Rebekah felt that the only thing to do was to lie and encourage her son's deception. Sounds to me like the making of a comedy, a true comedy of errors, with very serious ramifications. If we take anything away from this, it is simply to be honest. The honest truth is that we are not perfect. But we have a God who makes us perfect through his Son. So let's avoid the drama and just tell the truth.

- Where and when are you more prone to lie?

Pray: Lord, I confess that I am not always honest with you and others. Help me be truthful with those around me—and with you.

Jacob—I Must Be Dreaming

❖

He had a dream in which he saw a stairway resting on the earth, with its top reaching to heaven, and the angels of God were ascending and descending on it.
GENESIS 28:12

Context: Genesis 28:10-17

Over the years, I have had some pretty wild dreams. These normally occur after a belly full of good, spicy food. I often dream that I've slept through an alarm, only to run to class or the pulpit in my pajamas. In high school, I had a dream that I was free-falling. When I woke, I realized I was suspended in midair from the top bunk. The only thing that had saved me was the military-corner style of bed-making that my parents had taught me.

Jacob had a wild dream. This dream has been the inspiration behind numerous artistic depictions and even a few songs that occupy the airwaves. Jacob was on his own for the first time and was undoubtedly feeling lonely and unsure of his future. God came to him in a dream, not just to remind him but *to show him* that God and his angels were with him.

What a glorious picture for us. When we feel that life has us on the run or we feel lonely, we can take comfort in the fact that God's angels are watching over us and protecting us. Jesus came down from heaven so that we could have heaven as a result of his sacrifice. That is not a dream but a reality.

- Think of a Bible passage that comforts you when you feel alone.

Pray: Jesus, teach me to trust you and to know that you are always with me.

Leah Versus Rachel

❖

Laban had two daughters; the name of the older was Leah, and the name of the younger was Rachel. Leah had weak eyes, but Rachel had a lovely figure and was beautiful.
GENESIS 29:16,17
Context: Genesis 29:13-20

Some celebrities seem to live by this motto: "Looks aren't everything; they are the only thing." Many people marry for looks. And yes, you should be attracted to your spouse or the person you date. However, if you make looks the driving force behind your choice, you will be fighting an uphill battle. There is no fountain of youth. Eventually the effects of aging take over and you are left looking in the mirror not liking what you see. If looks determine whom you date or marry, what then?

Jacob's willingness to work for Rachel was noble. Maybe he put too much emphasis on her looks. Maybe he didn't. The Bible doesn't really tell us. But it does help us see that if we judge by looks, we might be making a serious mistake.

God blesses people in different ways: some with looks, some with personality, some with special gifts, and some with lasting legacies, etc. Leah, the lesser in Jacob's eyes, was blessed with sons, one of whom was the ancestor of the promised Savior. Yes, looks are important, but they are not the only thing. Love for God and gratitude for his blessings trump all.

- What measurement do you use when you evaluate other people?

- How does this influence the way you value other people?

Pray: Lord, help me to know that whether I see it or not, I am beautiful in your eyes—and truly blessed.

Laban the Liar

❖

"I served you for Rachel, didn't I? Why have you deceived me?"
GENESIS 29:25

Context: Genesis 29:21-30

This sentence has stuck with me: "You can pick your friends, but you can't pick your family." Simply put, you are stuck with your family. For many of you who are reading this, your family may provide a trouble-free zone for you. If so, say a prayer of thanks to God. Others of you may bear the scars left by the emotional or physical hurt inflicted by a family member. If this is the case, my heart goes out to you. Being hurt by a friend is one thing, but being hurt by someone who shares the same bloodline can have a lasting impact on your psyche.

Jacob was duped into working seven years for his Uncle Laban. Then, on Jacob's wedding night, Laban pulled a switcheroo in order to get more work out of Jacob. Lovestruck Jacob went along with the bargain and worked seven more years. After Jacob had endured Laban's shenanigans for more than 20 years, God told Jacob to return to his homeland. So he packed up to leave. Obviously, this upset Laban—his gravy train was heading out of town. However, God had blessed Laban through Jacob, and now it was time for the next chapter in Jacob's life to begin.

Those of us who have been hurt by our own blood relatives can remember the blood of our Savior Jesus that bleeds red for us. He has made us part of God's royal family. Like Jacob, you are blessed no matter what family issues you have experienced. No lies—one hundred percent truth—God loves you!

- What is ironic about the fact that Jacob was deceived?

Pray: Jesus, thank you for making me part of your family. Help me learn to forgive those who have hurt me.

Joseph's Arrogance

❖

Joseph had a dream, and when he told it to his brothers, they hated him all the more.
GENESIS 37:5
Context: Genesis 37:2-5

It is hard to be in a conversation—or even in a room—with someone who likes to talk only about themselves. An older sitcom made this point in a humorous way. One of the show's characters ran into a guy at the gym who always started his sentences with his own first name: "Jimmy loves to play basketball; Jimmy thinks you are cute." Though it was funny, it does bring home the point that no one likes a self-absorbed know-it-all.

Joseph was gifted in many ways. God also blessed him by giving him some amazing dreams. (Must run in the family.) Now, common sense would tell us to keep the contents of these dreams to ourselves. Not Joseph. He let his whole family know about these dreams. What was he expecting, a pat on the back? What he got was contempt and hatred from his siblings.

Our takeaway from this lesson has to do with humility. As shocking as it may be to hear, we are not God's gift to the world. Yes, God has gifted each of us with talents—some of us with amazing talents. What we do with those talents is our gift given back to God. God's gift to this world was his Son, who gifted us with eternal life. Let's use the lives we have and the gifts we have received in humble service to our God.

- What is the difference between arrogance and confidence?

- How can we make sure we have a proper attitude toward the gifts God has given us?

Pray: Jesus, forgive me for not always showing Christlike humility.

Sibling Rivalries

❖

**His brothers were jealous of him, but his father
kept the matter in mind.**
GENESIS 37:11
Context: Genesis 37:5-11

It is no surprise that the youngest child in a family is considered the favorite child. I am just speaking from experience. Mom and Dad spent all their time and effort teaching discipline to my older siblings. By the time I came along, I could do no wrong. It didn't hurt that my slightly older brother was a stinker; so compared to him, I was a saint. Certainly, neither my parents nor my siblings nor I were perfect. There were fights. Sadly, there are still disagreements that end up with me cynically being called "the chosen one" or the "highly favored one." When it seems that another person is being favored, there is always the temptation toward jealousy. This happens not just in families but also out in the real world. If a coach or teacher or member of the opposite sex gives attention or shows kindness to someone other than us, do we immediately react with happiness for the other person or do we react with jealousy and perhaps even hatred?

Joseph's brothers were no different. Jacob made no secret of the fact that his favorite wife had a favorite child and it wasn't one of them. Instead of looking at all the blessings they had, they went after Joseph. Granted, Joseph stoked the fires of jealousy by boasting about his dreams in front of his brothers.

We need to understand that God loves all of us the same. He does bless us all in different ways. But instead of worrying about what we don't have, we should focus on how God HAS blessed us (no matter where we fall in the birth order).

- How do insecurities contribute to our jealousies?

Pray: Lord, help me to remember that you love me just as much as you love everyone else.

Blind Brothers

❖

They saw him in the distance, and . . . they plotted to kill him.
GENESIS 37:18
Context: Genesis 37:12-18

Talk to people who are doing hard time, and they will tell you that they didn't just wake up one day and decide that a life of crime was going to be their career path. Their fall may have started in high school with something as simple as snatching cash from their best friend's locker. Then it was shoplifting pants at the local department store. From there it progressed to stealing cars to robbing homes to . . . boom—jail cell. The same principle can be applied to the young unmarried couples who are sexually active. It may have progressed from petting to "How far can we push these boundaries?" to "Now the sky is the limit."

The tension was building for Joseph's brothers. They knew how much their father loved Joseph. They saw how much Joseph flaunted that colorful coat in their faces. Their anger hijacked good judgment. Their solution: kill their brother. They were like Cain (see Week 2 Day 2), who had let his jealousy blind him to common sense. Fortunately, one brother had enough brains to say, "Murder is wrong." However, they ended up selling their brother and then lying to their parents. How far down a path of evil their jealousy had led them.

Ask yourself a serious question: How far down the rabbit hole of sin are you? Has your sin blinded you to the truth? It is not too late to repent and receive God's healing forgiveness, which alone can bring back clearer vision. Don't wait; do it now!

- What sins threaten to drag you away from God?

- How does the reminder of Jesus' forgiveness give you strength?

Pray: Lord, open my eyes to see the sins that are leading me down the wrong path.

Joseph Versus Potiphar's Wife

❖

"How then could I do such a wicked thing and sin against God?"
GENESIS 39:9

Context: Genesis 39:1-10

Everyone wants to be part of the "in" crowd. No one wants to sit alone at lunch. Imagine that the call comes: You get the nod from Mr. or Miss Popular to sit at their table. However, once you are sitting among the elite, you realize that the only things that come out of their mouths are insults and cuts aimed at those at other tables. Will you continue to sit with the "cool" kids? Will you dismiss yourself and risk their rejection? This is your big break. Will you throw it all away? Wouldn't it be easier just to go along with it?

In our lesson, Joseph caught the eye of Potiphar's wife, but he would not go along with her scheme to be unfaithful. One day it just so happened that all the servants were gone. That left just Joseph and her. It was the perfect situation. No one would know. Joseph, however, knew that the God he served knows and sees all things. Joseph knew that what she was asking was a sin.

The devil likes to put us in similar situations where we think no one will know. God knows.

Joseph was not blinded by lust but by love—love for what God says is right. Some might have excused Joseph on the grounds that he had endured a lot. But Joseph realized that no matter what happened in his life, good or bad, and no matter what the cool or popular people did, it was not a license to sin.

- What would you be willing to give up to be popular?

Pray: Lord, give me the strength that Joseph had to resist temptation.

WEEK 10 DAY 3

Joseph in Prison

❖

While Joseph was there in the prison, the LORD was with him.
GENESIS 39:20,21
Context: Genesis 39:11-21

I remember being in trouble in high school for something that wasn't my fault. Someone threw a piece of chewing gum under the teacher's desk. The teacher stepped on it, and I got in trouble for laughing. NOT FAIR.

Joseph said no to an adulterous affair and his reward was prison. NOT FAIR.

God punishing us for what our sins deserve would be, of course, FAIR. However, he did something contrary to that. He punished his perfect Son. Because of his Son, we are freed from the prison of hell. That's amazing grace.

God still had plans for Joseph—big plans. His life certainly resembled a roller coaster. From favorite son to the bottom of cistern. From a slave in charge of Potiphar's household to jail, accused of attempted rape. Up and down, up and down. Through all of this, God was molding and shaping Joseph for the future he had in store for him—to save God's people, through whom a Savior would be sent.

Rest easy. Perhaps right now your life resembles a thrill ride with corkscrews of terror, loopty loops of joy, and dark tunnels of sorrow. Keep in mind that God works through all circumstances for your good and that he will work through whatever it is you are experiencing now. When in doubt, go back to the cross and be reminded of the ultimate ride God has in store for you in heaven. Hang in there when the curves come. Know that God is sitting right next to you, and enjoy the ride!

- How does our definition of fair differ from God's?

Pray: Lord, teach me to hold on to you during this ride we call life.

30

WEEK 11 DAY 1

Joseph and Work

❖

The warden paid no attention to anything under Joseph's care, because the LORD was with Joseph.
GENESIS 39:23
Context: Genesis 39:21-23

What would be your ideal job? When I put this question on one of my quizzes just for fun, the most popular answer was "to get paid for doing nothing." Ever since the fall into sin, the mere mention of work makes us cringe. But we can look at work in a different way. No matter where this devotion finds you employed—or unemployed—work can be viewed as worship.

Joseph was still in prison, but he was making the most of it. He was not complaining. Instead he was doing what he could in the situation at hand. As a result, he was turning more people's eyes toward God. Why was this Hebrew kid so different? God made him that way! God was in his heart. What a perfect way to evangelize.

The next time you have to work at something as simple as cleaning your room, finishing your geometry assignment, making sure all those weeds are pulled, or cleaning both bathrooms, look at it as an opportunity to witness. Everyone expects you to grumble and complain. If you don't, you will be showing love and respect for your bosses and your parents. Ultimately, it will show others the love and respect you have for God.

Jesus didn't think twice when he washed his disciples' feet, even though his suffering and death were looming on the horizon. He washed their feet as an example for us to follow. Be like Jesus and Joseph. Follow their leads, and use the work you do as a way to worship the God who has saved us.

- In what ways can you approach your work as worship today?

Pray: Lord, thank you for giving me the abilities to work and to serve you. Use me to give witness to your love through the work I do.

31

Joseph—Bringer of News

❖

**"We both had dreams," they answered,
"but there is no one to interpret them."**
GENESIS 40:8

Context: Genesis 40:1-23

I've got good news, and I've got bad news. Which would you like to hear first? Joseph could have led off with that pitch to the baker and wine tester who were with him in jail. The interpretation of the baker's dream was bad news. It meant that his life was going to be ending soon. The wine tester? God still had plans for him—plans that included forgetting about Joseph until the time was right.

Joseph could have lied to the baker and told him what he wanted to hear. Instead he told the truth, good or bad.

We recognize this sign of a true friend: they stab us in the front instead of the back. They may tell us something we don't want to hear but need to hear. What sin is your friend caught in? Are you caught in it too? Love for God compels us to look out for our brothers and sisters in Christ. Say something; do something. We may think it is loving to say nothing and to look the other way, but that is not being a true friend.

Joseph had eaten his fair share of humble pie, so he wasn't grandstanding for his audience.

He was telling the truth in love—something we can pick up on. God has given us the opportunity to share his good news with others. We call a sin a sin. And when there is repentance, we offer the good news of forgiveness in Jesus' name.

- What's the best way for us to be truthful and loving?

Pray: Lord, give me the courage to be a true friend and to speak the truth in love today.

Takes One to Know One

❖

**When two full years had passed,
Pharaoh had a dream.**

GENESIS 41:1

Context: Genesis 41:1-13

It takes one to know one! Well, that's the pot calling the kettle black. It takes a thief to catch a thief—these statements all pretty much express the same thing. No one is better at understanding or finding a wrongdoer than another wrongdoer. Today we flip that around and say, *It takes a dreamer to help a dreamer.*

My how Joseph's life had turned. Just when it looked like he might get a break, when there was a chance that he could get out of jail, the wine tester forgot about Joseph for TWO YEARS! Yet again, Joseph's response was to keep working and to remain faithful despite his circumstances. After a full 730 days, Pharaoh had a dream that no one could understand. This jogged the memory of the wine tester, and he brought Joseph to the rescue. Joseph's brothers had called him the dreamer. Now God would use the dreamer to interpret Pharaoh's dreams.

God has called you to be where you are right now. Even if you do not understand how, God can use the very life situations you are in to aid or to help others. Wherever you find yourself in the middle of your own 730 days, trust that God has a plan. Be patient. "He who did not spare his own Son, but gave him up for us all—how will he not also, along with him, graciously give us all things?" (Romans 8:32).

- Identify two people who may be experiencing struggles similar to your own to whom you can reach out.

Pray: Lord, teach me to see that the problems you send my way are yet another way that you turn me to your Word so that I can grow stronger in faith and are another way that you prepare me to help others through similar struggles.

WEEK 12 DAY 1

Joseph Gives Credit Where Credit Is Due

❖

"I cannot do it," Joseph replied to Pharaoh, "but God will give Pharaoh the answer he desires."

GENESIS 41:16

Context: Genesis 41:14-40

As a fan of superhero movies, I almost always stay to the end of the credits to watch the "sneak preview" or "Easter egg" of the next movie. Once I clocked the closing credits at nearly ten minutes. That was quite a list of people to acknowledge. It makes you realize just how many hands it takes to make the work light during a movie project. I mean come on, what would a movie be without a key grip or a gaffer? No matter, they are there—and they are thanked for their services.

In our lesson, Joseph's leadoff pitch to Pharaoh wasn't to tell his own story about how he was wrongfully accused. Nor did he start out on an action-movie path of vengeance. Instead, when Pharaoh asked him to interpret his dream, Joseph gave credit where credit is due—to God.

In a world where we like to thump our own chests and let people know how gifted we are, this is a great example of acknowledging that everything we have comes from God. Our looks, our finances, our ability to dribble a ball, our brains, our salvation—all from God.

When opportunities come your way and people acknowledge something you have done well, take a breath, smile, and say, "Thank you, God." "Hey, you played a great game last night!" "Your recital piece was breathtaking." Your answer: "Yes, God gave me the ability to do that." Thank you, God!

- What are some of the talents God has given you?

Pray: Lord, teach me to fight the urge to be self-centered. Instead, help me to center my praise on you.

From Prison to the Penthouse

❖

Pharaoh said to Joseph, "I hereby put you in charge of the whole land of Egypt."
GENESIS 41:41
Context: Genesis 41:17-43

"Make sure your seat belt is securely fashioned and your hands are inside the vehicle at all times—and enjoy your ride!" If you take a ride on a roller coaster, you hear these words. My first such ride was on my senior class trip to Great America. The roller coaster looped, corkscrewed through a tunnel, and then "wound down" with more corkscrews until we were back where we started. My head was spinning as I got off the ride—from dizziness and from excitement.

God gave Joseph an amazing ride. His life took him through loops, turns, and corkscrews. Through it all, Joseph understood that God was directing the ride, so when Pharaoh asked him to interpret his dream, Joseph was quick to give credit to God. Joseph could have said, "Buckle up, Pharaoh! I am going to tell you what's up." Instead, he acknowledged that God is the one who should get the credit. The clear interpretation amazed Pharaoh. Just like that he promoted Joseph to a position equivalent to that of prime minister in today's world. One minute Joseph was a prisoner. The next, he was second-in-command. How does that happen? The answer is simple: God.

God knows what is going on in your world right now. He's not some wizard-of-Oz, distant God who has no clue about what you are dealing with. Yes, there may be some twists and turns in your life and your head may spin because of what's going on. Friends, keep close to God, wrap his Word around yourself like a seat belt, and rest your hands securely in HIS—and enjoy the ride!

- What lesson is there for us in this devotion?

Pray: Lord, help me to trust your promise to work all for good through the ups and downs of life.

Joseph's Savings Account

❖

Joseph stored up huge quantities of grain.
GENESIS 41:49

Context: Genesis 41:46-57

Are you a spender or a saver? Take the following quiz and see:

1. It's payday. Do you: A. Pay back a loan to a friend? B. Hit the *Place Your Order* button for the Amazon order you've had in your cart all week?
2. It's date night. Do you: A. Purchase tickets at the local theater? B. Go all out for the 3-D theater with lounge chairs, popcorn, and Milk Duds?
3. It's time for a new cell phone. Do you: A. Wait for three months so that you can save up enough to buy the newest and best model? B. Go pick one up this afternoon?
4. It's time for a wardrobe change. Do you: A. Check the sales rack? B. Hit the new arrivals, looking for the latest fashions?
5. You find 20 dollars in your coat pocket. Do you say to yourself: A. I'll just keep this in my pocket? B. Guess I'll be getting lunch out after all?

Through God's guidance, Joseph saved. The famine was coming, and Joseph needed to prepare an entire nation. While the land produced good crops, he stored away the excess to be used for a time when the land would be plagued with a seven-year famine. With God's blessing, nations were spared.

God wants us to use the gift of money wisely. Investing in your own future and in God's kingdom work here on earth is not only practical but biblically wise. Spender or saver, our motivation is the fact that we have a *Savior* who rescued us from the famine caused by sin.

• In what ways are you a spender or a saver?

Pray: Lord, everything I have from you is a gift. Give me biblical wisdom to use these gifts wisely.

Joseph Grudgeless

❖

"It was not you who sent me here, but God."
GENESIS 45:8

Context: Genesis 45:1-8

What would you do? Though you've been dating someone for a while, your best friend convinces you to break up with him or her. "This person just isn't right for you." Out of respect for your friend's advice, you act. The next weekend your friend isn't able to hang out because of other plans. Then the news arrives: Your friend and your ex were seen holding hands at the movies. How betrayed would you feel? What would you do? Would you find ways to get even, to trash their names, to prove you are better?

Take a look at Joseph. His brothers sold him into slavery. That sort of thing tends to leave a bit of a sting. But time and the Lord's plan heal all. Joseph realized his shortcomings and how God used the school of hard knocks to teach him to be less self-centered and more God-centered. God used the strange path Joseph's life took to save his people and to carry out his plan to save us. This life lesson helped Joseph realize that time is short and that forgiveness is the best medicine.

When you hold a grudge, you are allowing that person to have power over you. Let go of your anger and let the healing medicine of the gospel be your motivation. If someone has wronged you, forgive them as God, in Jesus, has forgiven you. It does not mean forget. It also does not mean hold a grudge. Trust God's plan. Know that he will never break up with you or betray you.

- Why is it hard to forgive?

- Whom do you need to forgive?

Pray: Lord, forgive us our sins as we forgive those who sin against us.

Joseph's Reunion

❖

Israel said to Joseph, "Now I am ready to die, since I have seen for myself that you are still alive."
GENESIS 46:30
Context: Genesis 45:16-18; 46:5-7,26-30

My brother enlisted in the service when I was ten. Six years later, when he was coming home, I remember making a sign to welcome him back. I saw his truck pull in and he stepped out—a taller and more distinguished person. He certainly didn't look like the guy who used to throw blankets over my head and try smothering me in front of his girlfriends. I immediately jumped into his arms and hugged him. It was the strangest mix of emotions—joy, tears, and excitement.

Two times I would like to have been a fly on the wall: when Jacob first heard the news that Joseph was alive, and then again later when he actually saw Joseph face-to-face after nearly two decades. There had to have been joy, tears, and excitement.

This, my friends, is a little like the way I picture heaven. A joyous reunion. People you once thought were dead are alive! Jesus makes this reunion possible.

My older brother did come home from the service. However, in time God saw fit to take his life in a snowmobile accident. Though I still feel the sadness, I do know that a reunion awaits us. I know it will be joyful and exciting. As you are reading this, if your heart aches over a loss, remember that God knows, God cares, and God has a joyous reunion planned for you as well.

- What will be the best part of our reunions in heaven?

- Why is it especially meaningful that Jesus will be part of our reunions?

Pray: Lord, thank you for conquering death and making heaven a place of joyful reunions.

The Oppressed

❖

The Egyptians worked them ruthlessly.
EXODUS 1:14

Context: Exodus 1:6-14

How long is this going to last? You may ask that when you are forced to sit through some boring romantic drama or ridiculous action flick. Or you may say this when you see a new couple holding hands.

If you had been in Egypt, you would have heard the Israelites uttering these words, which the psalmist later incorporated into his song: "How long, LORD?" (Psalm 13:1). Some background: The party days that had characterized the time of Joseph were over. There was a new sheriff in town, and he didn't take kindly to those born of Jewish descent. To eradicate the problem, he oppressed them. They felt the wrath of Pharaoh and the brutality of the taskmasters.

Perhaps you feel that the weight of the world is on your shoulders. Maybe you are single and everyone else is dating. You ask, "How long, Lord, will I be single?" Or you keep praying for God to give a specific solution to a challenge you are facing, but he says NO. And you ask, "HOW LONG, LORD?"

God may have allowed the Israelites to be oppressed so that they would long to go home to the Promised Land. The Israelites had lived in Egypt for 430 years—much of that time in slavery. A long time had passed, but God would deliver them.

God has also delivered us, who were slaves to sin, with the blood of his Son. We can be confident that God knows what we need. He has plans and a purpose for us, and he will govern our lives in order to carry out that purpose. Instead of asking how long, we say, "Your will be done!"

- What's the key to being patient?

Pray: Jesus, thank you for delivering me from the oppression of sin. When I'm tempted to ask, "How long?" teach me instead to trust in you.

WEEK 14 DAY 1

The Midwives

❖

The midwives, however, feared God and did not do what the king of Egypt had told them to do.

EXODUS 1:17

Context: Exodus 1:5-22

Do the names Kelly Rowland and Michelle Williams ring a bell? They didn't have the spotlight on them, but they were the women lending background harmonies to help Beyoncé start her career and provide her fun music. Without their vocals, there would have been no Destiny's Child. Without their vocals, Beyoncé might not have become famous.

Do the names Shiphrah and Puah sound familiar? These two Hebrew midwives were among the unsung, background heroes in Egypt. They were given a direct order to kill all the Hebrew boys when they were born. They knew murder was wrong. They also knew that following God was more important than obeying Pharaoh, so they disobeyed the executive order to commit genocide.

The consequence for them was not death by crocodiles in the Nile. God blessed them with families of their own.

Sometimes it's hard to stand up for the right thing. Perhaps a significant other is pressuring you to do what you know isn't right. Or a group of friends is trash-talking a teacher. May these two women be an inspiration to us when we struggle with the decision to do what is right versus what is popular. Yes, it may mean losing a friend or two, but trust that God has greater blessings in store.

- Why is it so hard to not follow the crowd?

Pray: Lord, help me see that following you, even when it isn't easy, is the right thing to do.

Moses' Mom, Sister, and Stepmom

❖

When she saw that he was a fine child, she hid him for three months. His sister stood at a distance to see what would happen to him. When the child grew older, she took him to Pharaoh's daughter and he became her son.

EXODUS 2:2,4,10

Context: Exodus 2:1-10

Tomb Raider depicts Lara Croft as a hero who travels around the world looking for lost artifacts and infiltrating hazardous tombs and dangerous ruins. Katniss Everdeen is another strong female character who doesn't always seem to have the odds ever in her favor. Lara and Katniss are inspirations for young people to be strong in the face of challenges or opposition. Today we meet three more heroes.

First, we see Moses' mom. She defied king and country to keep her son alive for as long as she could. Whether you realize it or not, your own mom is probably a lot like her. She loves and cares about you and will do anything for you.

The second character we meet is Moses' sister. She loved her brother and watched over him to make sure he was cared for. You can learn things from Miriam about how to show love and concern for your siblings.

Finally, we encounter Pharaoh's daughter. She valued human life more than obedience to her father's orders.

But the real hero is the one who cherishes the forgiveness that is his or hers in Jesus and is determined to honor him with his or her life, even when the world's values are very different.

- Define strength.

Pray: Lord, give me the wisdom to recognize and emulate the values that serve you.

Moms Connect Us to Jesus

❖

Pharaoh's daughter said to her, "Take this baby and nurse him for me, and I will pay you." So the woman took the baby and nursed him.
EXODUS 2:9

Context: Exodus 2:5-10

What is the first Bible story you remember hearing as a child? How about the first Bible song you learned? Who told you that story or taught you that song? Was it perhaps a parent, a grandparent, or a teacher? Our reading today shows how God arranged for Moses to remain in the care of his God-fearing mother for a time. Though the biblical account is very brief, it is evident that before she gave him up permanently, she had been feeding him not only physically but also spiritually. From what happened later in Moses' life, it is obvious that his mother had taught him that he was one of God's people, a Hebrew. She had taught him about the God of their fathers. She had planted the seed that took root in his heart before he was subjected to the false gods of Egypt.

The Bible encourages parents today to do the same. "Start children off on the way they should go, and even when they are old they will not turn from it" (Proverbs 22:6).

My children love to play with Legos. I have to keep reminding them that before building the tower, they need to have a good solid base; otherwise, the tower will tip and maybe even collapse.

If you do not have a good spiritual base, you, like the Lego tower, will topple. Parents, teachers, and pastors encourage you to stay in God's Word. Doing so will prepare you to be able to stand tall and not be blown over by the struggles of life.

- Think of specific spiritual struggles that require you to keep building your life on the solid foundation of God's Word.

Pray: Lord, thank you for giving me caring adults who taught me the truths of your Word.

Moses—Penthouse to Poorhouse

❖

Moses fled from Pharaoh and went to live in Midian.
EXODUS 2:15

Context: Exodus 2:11–22

Everyone loves a rags-to-riches story. But how about when the opposite happens? In the blink of an eye, Moses went from enjoying the perks of being the son of Pharaoh's daughter to shoveling sheep dung in the hill country of Midian.

What went wrong? God was not ready for Moses to lead just yet. Much like the anxious child who wants to pull the cookies out of the oven before they are fully cooked, Moses had jumped the gun in his desire to save his people. But God's timer had not yet sounded.

Moses needed some more training. Sure, he had had the best teachers money could buy while he was growing up in Egypt; what more could Moses need? Like Joseph before him, God was working to give Moses a dash of patience and humility. In addition, God was getting him familiar with the land through which he would later lead God's people.

God works that way, doesn't he? Last year's star of the play doesn't even make the chorus this year. The player who can't miss a shot in one game can't hit the broadside of a barn in the next. Through it all, God teaches us the same life lessons of patience and humility. God's goal is not to shame us but to build us up and get us ready for the next adventure.

Because we are God's children through Jesus, we can trust that all of our life lessons are for our good.

- How has God taught you patience and humility?

Pray: Lord, teach me to rely on you when things don't go the way I would like.

God Calls Moses

❖

God called to him from within the bush.

EXODUS 3:4

Context: Exodus 3:1–12

How do you act when you are expecting an important call or text? Do you pace around the room, checking the phone every 30 seconds? Why do you do that? You don't want to miss the call.

For the previous 40 years in Midian, Moses had put his phone on silent. During this time, his life and focus had changed from imagining himself as a savior and leader of his people in Egypt to being a sheep farmer and family man. He didn't realize what God had been preparing him to do. Finally, after all of those years, God called him in a very unique way to let him know that it was time for him to step up and lead.

Perhaps life, a relationship, or a sporting season has not gone as you had intended. Even if it seems God has forgotten you, know for sure that he has not. Take heart that God has plans for you and has called you. He called you by the gospel to be his dear child. And he calls you to serve him in your own unique way, with your own unique gifts. The call might not be to serve as a leader like Moses. It may be to provide for your family as a faithful father or mother or to let the gospel shine in your life while you serve as a humble employee. Each unique service is a part of his plan and his kingdom work.

The phone is ringing—pick it up. You do not want to miss this call!

• To what mission field is God calling you?

Pray: Lord, thank you for calling me to be your servant. Use me today to tell others about you.

WEEK 15 DAY 3

Moses and His Excuses

❖

**Moses said, "Pardon your servant, Lord.
Please send someone else."**
EXODUS 4:13
Context: Exodus 4:1-17

What is your go-to excuse when you mess up? The dog ate my homework? Traffic was a bear? My car won't start? I just came down with a rare illness? Moses looked for excuses when God called him. But God silenced each of his fears.

Moses' first excuse was, "They won't believe me!" God's answer was to give him three miraculous signs: a staff that turned into a snake, the ability to turn water into blood, and a leprous hand. Still not convinced, Moses went to excuse number two: "I am slow of speech and tongue."

God's answer: "I will help you speak."

Finally, Moses admitted that he just didn't want to do it: "Send someone else." God's answer was that Aaron would be Moses' spokesman.

Three excuses—three comforting responses from God.

So where is God asking you to go or what is he asking you to do? Reach out to that neighbor? Bring up Christ to your non-Christian friends? Reconnect with that wayward sibling? As he did for Moses, God gives us signs of his love. In the miracles of Baptism and the Lord's Supper, we are reminded of who we are and what God has done for us. God gives us special gifts and talents to serve him. God reminds us in his Word that he is *always* with us. God also sends fellow believers to encourage us on this mission we call life. So what is your excuse?

- How does the knowledge that God uses imperfect people serve as a source of comfort for you?

Pray: Lord, quiet my excuses by filling my heart with faith to trust your plans for my life.

The Passover

❖

"It is the Passover sacrifice to the Lord, who passed over the houses of the Israelites in Egypt and spared our homes when he struck down the Egyptians."
EXODUS 12:27
Context: Exodus 12:1-13,24-27

What is your favorite holiday? I love Easter because the days are getting longer, it is getting warmer in my zip code, and school is almost out. Without a doubt, no matter what holiday you happen to pick as your favorite, you will have to mention the food. What holiday is complete without home cooking, desserts, and, of course, family?

God instructed the Israelites to celebrate what would become a major holiday: the Passover. For the Passover, the main course was lamb. Like Grandma's homemade apple pie, which needs ingredients and follows a recipe, God prescribed the ingredients for the Passover meal and gave the Israelites the recipe. It was to be a lamb without blemish or defect. And the blood of this lamb was to be sprinkled on the door posts. It was the blood of the lamb that would spare them when the angel of death passed over their homes.

It is the blood of Jesus, the Lamb of God, that frees you from your sins and from eternal death. As you read this, you may feel you are being held captive by a specific sin. Rest easy. You are in a good family—God's family. There is another reason Easter is my favorite—the empty tomb. Like the blood that covered those Israelite doorposts, the blood of Jesus covers us. How can we be so sure? The empty tomb seals the deal that we are no longer dead in our sins but have forgiveness, peace, and life.

- What holidays have Christian significance?

- Why is that significance important to you?

Pray: Lord, thank you for being the Lamb of God who takes away the sin of the world.

God Gives Daily Bread

❖

The LORD said to Moses, "I will rain down bread from heaven for you."

EXODUS 16:4

Context: Exodus 16:1-8

There is something special about the experience of walking into your home and your nose immediately being hit with the aroma of freshly baked bread. Whether it was baked in the oven or a bread maker, you just slap on a little butter, some jam or honey, and you have yourself a mouthful of deliciousness. Some could eat a whole loaf in one sitting.

God provided daily bread for the Israelites in the desert. Manna fell from the sky for them to eat. What a miracle!

God provides us with daily bread. Granted, it does not fall from the sky, but our closets and fridges are full of the daily blessings we receive from God. For this, we say thank you!

In time the people of Israel learned to complain even about the gifts they received directly from heaven. Do we complain about our blessings too? The phone, the car, and the wardrobe are all outdated. Worse yet, you open the fridge and (gasp) the only things in there are leftovers. It is easy to fall into the complain cycle and to act and sound as if God has shafted us. Instead, let's take a thanksgiving inventory and look at the ways God has blessed us, rather than focusing on what we don't have. Let's remember especially that Jesus endured the suffering we deserved so that we can have the treasures of heaven. When you flip your mind-set and acknowledge that you are indeed blessed by God, you can enjoy the fresh aroma of a blessed life!

- I am grateful for . . .

Pray: Lord, thank you for giving us today our daily bread!

Aaron and Peer Pressure

❖

He took what they handed him and made it into an idol cast in the shape of a calf, fashioning it with a tool. EXODUS 32:4

Context: Exodus 32:1-20

In a popular Christmas movie, a small child is double-dog dared to stick his tongue to an ice-cold pole in the middle of winter. If you have ever done something like that, you know how dumb you feel as you wait for your tongue to heal.

Most of us could probably write a book about the dumb stuff we've done. Begging an answer is the prevailing question: why did you do it? There is something to be said about peer pressure. If someone is watching, males especially seem to feel the need to "man up" and do things we normally would not do.

Aaron was in charge while Moses was on the mountain getting God's laws. What happened is mind-boggling. Aaron—the priest, mind you—was peer pressured into giving the people what they wanted: a false god to worship. This was a god Aaron made with his own hands. I wonder if at any time while he was doing this, he asked himself, "What am I doing?"

For us, peer pressure is real. Friends, significant others, and even just the longing to fit in may make the wisest of us do or try stupid things. When we do these stupid things, we are blessed to know that Jesus took our sinful acts upon himself when he went to the cross.

The lesson to learn here is to remember that there is power in the word *no!* Say no when friends or others want you to try something that dishonors God.

- In what areas of your life do you feel pressure to do things that you know aren't right?

- What steps can we take to avoid giving in?

Pray: Lord, forgive me for giving in to peer pressure. Give me the strength to say no next time.

Israel Equals Uncle Rico

❖

**"We remember the fish we ate in Egypt at no cost—
also the cucumbers, melons, leeks, onions and garlic.
But now we have lost our appetite;
we never see anything but this manna!"** NUMBERS 11:5,6

Context: Numbers 11:4-10

In the movie *Napoleon Dynamite,* one character in particular brought humor to the screen. Uncle Rico was a traveling Tupperware salesman whose attire looked like it was stolen from the 1970s. What made Uncle Rico comical was that he loved to talk about the good old days. He wasn't shy about telling anyone how good he was at football back in the day and that he would do anything to go back to those days.

The people of Israel suffered from what I call *UncleRicoitis.* When a challenge came their way, they pushed the whine button and lamented about the good old days and how they wished they were back in Egypt. Hello, people! You were slaves in Egypt. The good old days were not that good. How soon they forgot.

Perhaps you are stuck in a rut in your life. What is your solution? Do you look back, or do you look forward? Perhaps you got out of a relationship that was detrimental to your faith walk. But now, as time has passed and loneliness is weighing you down, you are feeling the pull to go back.

Yes, it is great to study the past and learn from it. However, the past is the past. You can't go back—you can't change it. What you can do is move forward, take that leap of faith, and walk forward with the Lord, knowing that he has forgiven your sins and is with you every step of the way.

- What lessons does the past teach us?

- What cautions should we be aware of as we think about the past?

Pray: Lord, teach me to keep my eyes focused on you!

A Rememberer

❖

"Remember the Sabbath day."
EXODUS 20:8

Context: Exodus 20:1–17

The confirmation student stood at the front of the church, sweat pouring down his face. He couldn't think of the answer to the question the pastor had just asked. The question: "Please give me a commandment that reminds us to keep God's day holy." (Keep in mind how the Third Commandment begins.) After the long pause, the pastor said, "Clark, . . . remember . . ." To which I responded, "No." Then he said, "No, Clark, . . . remember the . . ." And then I got it. I said, "Remember the Sabbath day by keeping it holy."

Why did I go blank in front of the congregation? Because I was worried I would have a dry mouth when I spoke, I had asked my Mom for some breath mints. Instead of putting a few in my pocket, I was carrying three complete packs. When I walked, it sounded like I was in a Western movie and my spurs were jingling. The laughs from the congregation as they puzzled over the noise made the mind of this St. Peter's Hawk (our mascot) go blank.

Fast forward to you. What makes your mind go blank when it comes to remembering God's Word? Life, work, dating, friends—these can all be blessings. But the devil will try to convince you to put them in your front pocket and to rely on them to give meaning to your life. As you sit in church and worship God, you are reminded that those things can be distractions if you let them. Take the time out of your day to remember his Word. You will hear some wonderful promises. You will hear of the gift of eternal life that Jesus has won for you, which is the most valuable treasure of all. Listen to his Word, and say thank you!

• What distractions do you have in your life?

Pray: Lord, remind me to remember you daily.

Spies Like Us

❖

The LORD said to Moses, "Send some men to explore the land of Canaan, which I am giving to the Israelites."
NUMBERS 13:1,2

Context: Numbers 13:1,2,21-33

I am a fan of a certain British spy who goes by the name of 007. Though many different actors have played the title role, the truth remains that 007 is the best that British intelligence has to offer. He goes on the deadliest missions in the most exotic locations using the most extraordinary gadgets; and in the end, he always wins.

Moses sent out 12 spies to scout out the land of Canaan. Their mission was to report on the land and to get the people fired up about the land God was about to give them. It was a way of assuring the people that with God going in front of them, they would always be winners. Only two spies believed they could take the land because God was on their side. The other ten spies had no faith. They agreed that the land was great. But when they had seen the people who lived there, their hearts melted in fear. Their cowardly report triggered another whine fest among the people of Israel.

In your mission in life, which spy report do you believe? When a challenge rises up in your personal life, do you follow the ten, believing your situation is hopeless? Or do you trust that God can and will get you through it? Which mission will you choose? Remember God's promise: "He who did not spare his own Son, but gave him up for us all—how will he not also, along with him, graciously give us all things?" (Romans 8:32).

- What gets in the way of our mission of trusting God?

Pray: Lord, teach me that no matter what my mission in life may be, you are always working things out for my good!

Joshua

❖

**"Have I not commanded you?
Be strong and courageous.
Do not be afraid; do not be discouraged,
for the LORD your God will be with you
wherever you go."**
JOSHUA 1:9

Context: Joshua 1:1-9

What is your confirmation verse? The verse above graces many a plaque or graduation invite. It is very fitting for anyone embarking on a new adventure in life. It is also a popular confirmation verse. Joshua had been a military leader under Moses for more than 40 years. He had watched as Moses led. Now Moses was gone. It was up to him to lead. And don't forget what kind of people he had to lead. The motto of the people of Israel seemed to be, "When the going gets tough, we start complaining." So here he was, managing a group of people whose claim to fame seemed to be that they loved to whine. But instead of letting Joshua stew or fret over the prospect of leading such people, the Lord was there as his spiritual cheerleader with a message of tremendous comfort. If you are having one of those days when it seems like the world is against you or you are facing a change or a challenge in life, read the first nine verses of Joshua and know that God is speaking directly to you! Do you know why you can be absolutely certain these words apply to you? Because Jesus has forgiven all of your sins. Nothing can separate you from his love.

• What keeps you from being strong and courageous?

Pray: Lord, only with you can I be strong and courageous. Keep your promise to be with me wherever I go.

Rahab

❖

So [the two spies] went and entered the house of a prostitute named Rahab and stayed there.
JOSHUA 2:1

Context: Joshua 2:1-21

When you look in the mirror, do you like what you see? Perhaps you are plagued by memories from the past and, as much as you try, you can't shake the memories of sins you have committed. Sometimes that guilt can cripple your thinking, leaving you to conclude that you are worthless.

Friends, see Exhibit A or, in this case, Exhibit RAHAB. Though she was a prostitute, God had big plans for her. Lest you think the author is condoning her lifestyle, know this: he is not! However, what he does want you to see is that God can use any of us—any sinner—to carry out his will. Rahab became a savior to the spies. She helped them escape the king's soldiers so they could continue their mission. As compensation for her kindness, with a scarlet cord, her family was spared when Israel destroyed Jericho. And her story did not end there. If you have any interest in genealogies and tracing family trees, it might interest you to know that from the family line of this savior of the spies came the Savior of all nations. Wow, imagine that. Her past sins did not define her. She made a change, and God forgave her. And purely out of his grace, God made her family name something to be remembered.

We struggle with sin. We struggle with the past. Take heart, my friends, because your past sins do not define you either. God forgives you and has big plans for you. Trust him whose scarlet red blood covers all of your sins!

- What past sins still haunt you?

Pray: Lord, help me to bask in your forgiveness and to trust the future plans you have for me.

Joshua Loves Worship

❖

"As for me and my household, we will serve the LORD."
JOSHUA 24:15

Context: Joshua 24:1-15

The older Joshua had seen a whole generation turn their backs on God and die. Joshua knew very well that success comes from the hand of God alone.

When you stay close to God, your life has meaning and purpose. Many of us understood that when we were little. Then we grew up and "got smart." Then the devil tried to lure us away from God and to get us to think that we don't need God or that his Word is outdated and not important.

"Pastor's sermons are boring." "It's a waste of time; I have better things to do."

The devil wants nothing more than for you to turn your back on God and his Word.

Think about these three things: a computer, a car, and a cell phone. What do they all have in common? What do they need to run? The car and cell phone each need a battery. The computer needs a source of electricity. Without a power source, the machines are useless and die. Your faith is the same way. It needs its battery charged, and that comes solely from the Word of God. My encouragement for you is to realize that God forgives us for the times we've neglected his Word. Let his forgiveness encourage you to make an effort to stay plugged in to the Word. Come to Bible class, and make it a priority to encourage your friends to do the same. Say with the psalmist, "I rejoiced with those who said to me, 'Let us go to the house of the LORD'" (Psalm 122:1). Say with Joshua, "As for me and my household, we will serve the LORD."

- Think of three reasons teens don't read their Bibles or don't feel that Bible class is worthwhile.

Pray: God, fill me with your Spirit so I stay plugged in to you.

Gideon Trusts in God

❖

**Gideon sent the rest of the Israelites home
but kept the three hundred.**
JUDGES 7:8

Context: Judges 6:1–16; 17:1–23

When you hear the number 300, what thoughts come to mind? One might think of King Leonidas of Sparta and his force of three hundred men who fought the Persians at Thermopylae in 480 B.C. While this battle could be turned into a great Hollywood blockbuster, you might say that this was actually a sequel to something that happened in biblical times.

The book of Judges has a very cyclical plot. Israel follows the Lord. Israel falls away from the Lord. The Lord sends a rival nation to oppress Israel. Israel cries out to the Lord, and the Lord sends a judge to deliver the nation of Israel. In this case, God sent Gideon. So Gideon is the protagonist, and the antagonist is the nation of Midian. By whittling down Gideon's army to just three hundred men, God taught Gideon a very important lesson. Do not put your trust in human wisdom or power but only in the Lord. God used Gideon and his brave three hundred soldiers to defeat the huge Midianite army with ease.

Perhaps the plot of your personal movie is at a point of high drama. Maybe you feel the oppression of stress and deadlines and of loneliness—and you feel defeated. Take heart, dear Christian, God is more powerful. The same God who could defeat a vast army with a force only a small fraction of that army's size can overpower whatever it is that we struggle with. God gave Gideon proof after proof that he was behind him. Continue to look through the pages of Scripture to remind yourself daily that the God who went to battle with Gideon is the same God who walks side by side with you.

• How do you define *trust?*

Pray: Lord, help me to trust you no matter what army I face today.

WEEK 19 DAY 2

Samson's Strength

❖

The Spirit of the LORD came powerfully upon him
so that he tore the lion apart with his bare hands
as he might have torn a young goat.
JUDGES 14:6

Context: Judges 14:1-9

Every so often I catch a show on the cable sports network called *The World's Strongest Man Competition*. If you have never seen this show, you might find it worth a look. You will see guys whose necks and arms are the size of my waist. These muscle-bound men have to complete a number of challenging tasks to prove their strength. These tasks include lifting and carrying a hollowed-out VW Beetle car 35-40 yards or throwing kegs of beer over a ten foot wall. Whoever can complete all of the tasks is dubbed the "strongest man."

Long before there were cable TV networks, we met another strong man. His name was Samson. He was Israel's strongest man. His feats included carrying off the doors of the city gate, killing wild animals with his bare hands, tying fox tails together to create a bonfire in the fields of the Philistines, and more.

The source of Samson's strength? It was not in his biceps or his NFL linebacker hair. It was in the Lord. God used Samson and his strength to bring the hearts of the Israelites back to him.

God equips you with many talents. Granted, you may not be lifting doors, but you can be lifting people's hearts with a kind word. Maybe you are not setting fires to a field, but perhaps you are on fire to help others. An important truth to remember is that God does not give us tasks equal to our strength, but he gives us the strength equal to our tasks.

- What are your strengths?

Pray: Lord, help me to see you as the only source of my strength.

Samson's Weakness

❖

Delilah said to Samson, "Tell me the secret of your great strength and how you can be tied up and subdued."
JUDGES 16:6

Context: Judges 16:4-22

It is not uncommon to glance at the local tabloid magazines and see headlines that talk about the blunders of famous athletes or stars. A star quarterback with many Super Bowl trophies is found to have a mistress. An actor who has the world by the tail and is constantly mobbed by throngs of screaming, adoring fans overdoses. Many of these stories shock us. However, are they really anything new?

Look at Samson. While I admire Samson, he did have his faults. True, he was strong and a great defender of Israel. However, his pride and his poor choice in women contributed to his downfall.

Delilah worked for the enemy, but Samson was too lovestruck or blinded by pride to see it.

As a result, he took his focus off of the one who gave him his strength.

But Samson's story hits a little closer to my heart than I might want to admit. It does for most of us. One minute you might be the star at school, at work, or in your family. But you take your eye off the ball just for a minute, and the devil swoops in to pump your ego. Then you say goodbye to common sense and eagerly embrace sin. You take that sip of booze, try a little pot, go a little farther on your date.

Samson experienced serious consequences for his actions. It is no different for us. Fortunately, we have in Jesus a Savior who took the sin of our pride to the cross and soundly defeated our enemy.

- What is your weakness?

Pray: Lord, when I am successful, work humility in my heart so I realize that all I have is a gift from you.

Samson—The Conclusion

❖

The Philistines . . . gouged out his eyes and . . . set him to grinding grain in the prison. But the hair on his head began to grow again.
JUDGES 16:21,22
Context: Judges 16:21-30

In the *Star Wars* movie series, Anakin's story is bittersweet. This small boy grows to be the strongest Jedi, but then he turns to the dark side and becomes the most iconic cinematic villain of the past century. Just before he dies, however, his son brings him back to the light.

Samson's story follows a similar path. Samson is now blind and working as the Philistines' mule and source of entertainment. This piece of humble pie gives him time to think about his actions and to repent and turn back to his only source of strength—God.

In the end, Samson regains his strength and God grants his request to do what he was called to do: protect the people of Israel from the hands of the Philistines. Samson's death was not a suicide, as the death of a soldier who jumps on the grenade to save his platoon is not a suicide.

Some of us reading this have been plagued by mistakes that resulted when we allowed our pride to push God into the back seat, and we turned to the dark side of sin. Perhaps God has humbled us in order to wake us up. God forgave Samson, and God forgives you! You can be confident that Jesus has knocked down the pillars—the devil, the world, and our sinful natures—that were in our way. He alone brings you from the dark into the light.

- Agree or disagree: Samson was right to do what he did. Why or why not?

- From Samson's story, what do you learn about God's care of his people?

Pray: Lord, thank you for assuring me that all my dark-side sins are forgiven.

Hannah

❖

**Each year his mother made him a little robe and
took it to him when she went up with her husband
to offer the annual sacrifice.**

1 SAMUEL 2:19

Context: 1 Samuel 1:20-28; 2:19-21

As a child, the highlight of every fall was going school supply shopping with my mom. Love was found in the school supply aisle, picking up #2 pencils, *Dukes of Hazzard* folders, and an *Empire Strikes Back* lunchbox.

Even today in my "seasoned" years, my mother and I make a day of shopping for an outfit before school starts.

Hannah had been unable to have children. God heard her prayer and answered it with the birth of Samuel. Her response to this blessing? She gave her son back to God and allowed him to live away from home.

Hannah loved her son, but she knew that her child was really God's. As a student, I attended and lived at a boarding high school that was only eight miles from my home. People would often ask my parents, "Why would you send your kids away at age 14?" My parents' answer was a witness to their faith: "Sure he is our son, but he is really God's."

What a remarkable reminder for us that the blessings we have—people or possessions—are all on loan from God. That also applies to the caring adults in our lives. People and possessions are temporary. What is eternal is God and his love for you.

- How does this truth that all we have is on loan from God affect our decisions?

Pray: Lord, thank you for giving me caring adults to mentor me.

WEEK 20 DAY 3

Samuel

❖

Samuel said, "Speak, for your servant is listening."
1 SAMUEL 3:10

Context: 1 Samuel 3:1-10

If you had visited our home during the time my wife was pregnant, you might have been met by an odd scene: me sitting on our couch and talking to . . . her belly. It has been proven that children in the womb can recognize the voices of their parents, so I wanted to make sure the baby heard my voice.

On an average day, teenagers hear many voices. In addition to parents, they hear the voices of teachers, bus drivers, siblings, and employers, as well as the robotic voices on their electronic devices. Which of those voices captures your attention the most? The world we live in is screaming with so much noise. Sadly, we get stuck listening to those voices. Voices that encourage us to look down on others. Voices that remind us of our past sins. Some days the volume seems to be turned all the way up. When these moments come, turn off the TV, tune out the rambling voices on social media, and just say, "Speak, Lord!"

Young Samuel was listening in the wrong place for the voice that was speaking to him. Sometimes we listen in the wrong places too. The Holy Spirit calls us by the gospel. When we realize that he works through the Word and sacraments, we are ready to say to our God, "Speak, Lord, I am listening." God's voice is the only voice that matters. It is the voice that is with us in life and the voice that will welcome us home to heaven. Turn it up!

- What are some of the distractions that drown out the voice of God for us?

Pray: Speak, Lord, as I come to you to listen to your Holy Word.

Samuel's Farewell

❖

**Samuel replied . . . "Be sure to fear the Lord
and serve him faithfully with all your heart;
consider what great things
he has done for you."**
1 SAMUEL 12:20,24
Context: 1 Samuel 12:20-25

The date is July 4, 1939, and Lou Gehrig is addressing thousands at Yankee Stadium.

The smell of freshly popped popcorn is in the air. Flashbulbs snap and crackle while the microphone echoes the famous words, "I consider myself the luckiest man on the face of the earth." Some believe this is one of the most heartfelt goodbyes ever spoken.

Long before baseball became America's pastime, the prophet Samuel addressed the people of Israel one last time. He too could have said he was the luckiest man alive or, more appropriately, the most blessed man who ever lived. The back of his baseball card would show his minor league time spent under Eli the priest. His stats would include anointing kings and faithfulness to God.

In his heartfelt goodbye, notice that Samuel didn't focus on his accomplishments as most athletes do today. Instead, he focused on where the credit is due, on God. Samuel wanted to remind the people of Israel one last time to keep their eyes focused on God.

Samuel's farewell reminds us that all our blessings as well as all our sufferings come from God. Lou Gehrig had to say farewell to a sport he loved because of an illness that would later take his life. Yet, he remained optimistic.

We can be optimistic like Samuel and like Gehrig. This optimism isn't found in any earthly accomplishments but rather in our loving Savior. We are truly blessed to know who Jesus is. We can look at his perfect stats and can see the sacrifice he made to make us his own.

- What makes saying goodbye hard? joyful?

Pray: Lord, as we face the trials of life, help us to stay focused not on ourselves but on our Savior!

David and Goliath

❖

This day the LORD will deliver you into my hands.
1 SAMUEL 17:46

Context: 1 Samuel 17:1-50

"How much do you trust me?" our teacher asked his students. Immediately, a friend and I shot up our hands and waved them so emphatically that we could have landed planes with all the arm motions. The two of us were chosen for the demonstration. Our teacher stood between us and told us to turn around and face away from him with our arms crossed. He then instructed my friend to fall backward with his arms crossed while I watched. As soon as my friend started to fall, my teacher caught him. After giving me the same instructions, he told me to fall backward. Only this time his hands were lower than when he caught my friend. You can probably imagine what happened next. Realizing that I was falling farther than my friend had, I panicked and put my hand out to catch myself. I, in fact, did not trust my teacher. Instead, I relied on my own reasoning and strength.

David was the only one in Israel who passed the trust-fall test. More than in the king and his entire army, he put his trust in God alone. With well-placed faith in the true God, he was confident that God would give him the victory.

Where do you put your trust? As you read this, into what are you falling backward? School, pressures, relationships, old sinful habits? Do you trust that God is stronger and able to take on our strongest foes? Even if you cannot see him, *he is there* ready to catch you!

• What prevents us from having childlike trust?

Pray: God, help me to trust you above my own reasoning.

David and Saul

❖

**"Don't destroy him! Who can lay a hand on
the Lord's anointed and be guiltless?"**

1 SAMUEL 26:9

Context: 1 Samuel 26:1-11

"R.E.S.P.E.C.T. Find out what it means to me" are the lyrics to a tune that sings of racial and gender equality. It is easy to give respect to those in our inner circle. We also show respect to those from whom we have something to gain. What about those we don't necessarily like? Or those with whom we do not associate? David was on the run, and he was being pursued by his father-in-law, the king. His crime? NOTHING! David was innocent. The time came when David could have taken Saul's life. But he did not. His respect for God's anointed king, whether the king was good or not, was greater than his own personal agenda. David taught his men a valuable lesson that day about respecting God and others.

Today that same lesson can be applied to us. There are people with whom we cross paths at work or school. Some you may get along with, and others you may not. In either case, all people are God's creation. We respect those around us even if they are not in our inner circle. If someone is gifted differently than we are, we still show them love and respect as a child of God, even if it is not reciprocated. Hard? Yes! Impossible? No! David seized a teachable moment and did not try to gain glory for himself but rather for the one who created all human life.

- Agree or disagree, and explain your answer: God wants us to forgive and forget.

Pray: Lord, teach me to find my worth in you and to treat others with respect.

David and Jonathan

❖

Jonathan said to David, "Go in peace, for we have sworn friendship with each other in the name of the Lord."

1 SAMUEL 20:42

Context: 1 Samuel 20:24-42

What is your definition of a friend? I once heard this given as the definition of a true friend: someone who stabs you in the front instead of in the back. Roughly translated, it means that a true friend may tell you something you don't *want* to hear but that you *need* to hear. Over the years, I have gained and lost many friends. Many times the losses came about when I was going through a crisis. Everybody loves you when you are the star of the class, the captain of the team, or the kid with the pool. What happens when you are cut from the team, your grades stink, or you are drowning in a pool of sorrow? Who is there for you then? During the darker times in life, our friendships face the litmus test and we find out who our true friends are.

David had a true friend named Jonathan. The sticky part of this friendship was that Jonathan was King Saul's son. Jonathan was next in line for the throne. However, God had other plans. David was his pick to be the next king. Other people in Jonathan's shoes would have resented David. Not Jonathan. He loved and protected David, because he knew that David as king was what God wanted.

Examine your friendships. Look for people like Jonathan who are more willing to give than to get. Jesus was and is our truest friend. He gave his very life for us. Look especially for people who believe in Jesus and who will be there to encourage you to trust in Jesus.

- List characteristics that define a friend.

Pray: What a friend we have in Jesus! Father, help me to model his love for my friends.

Solomon Gives Wisdom

❖

**Let the wise listen and add to their learning,
and let the discerning get guidance.**
PROVERBS 1:5

Context: Proverbs 1:1-7

Just before my senior year at the seminary, I was called to be an emergency tutor at the prep school I had attended. After my first year as tutor, they asked me back for a second year. As an undergraduate, I needed to seek the approval of the seminary, so I called one of my advisors to ask for permission. The conversation went something like this: "Hello, Professor. They have asked me to serve another year as a tutor."

He responded, "Well, Scott. If you feel this is where you need to be, Scott, then I feel, Scott, that it is the best thing for you." Though my name isn't Scott, I rolled with this conversation. Just after he had called me Scott for the fourth time, he stopped and said, "Your name isn't Scott."

"No, it is not, Professor," I said.

To which he said, "Do you know any Scotts?"

"No, I do not, Professor."

"Neither do I. Stay at Prep and enjoy another year." CLICK.

To this day, I am still uncertain if this professor, who was known for his sense of humor, was pulling my leg. However, having his blessing and counsel meant a great deal.

As you go through life, God places mentors in your life—people who give good counsel. Seek them out and listen to their God-given wisdom and Christian advice. The writer of Proverbs says that this is the mark of a wise person: they listen and get guidance.

- Make a list of people you can count on to help you with big decisions.

Pray: Lord, thank you for the many mentors you have put in my life.

WEEK 22 DAY 3

A Thankful Psalmist

❖

Give thanks to the LORD.
PSALM 107:1

Context: Psalm 107:1-43

The joy on my son's face is priceless on a Sunday morning. He's so excited when it's time to give our offering at church. He has the biggest smile in the world when he drops the white offering envelope in the plate.

As we get older, we tend to lose that joy toward giving. Perhaps we're sitting with some friends at a local fast-food restaurant when one of them reaches to grab one of our fries. What is our first reaction? "Yes, dear friend, what is mine is yours. Please take one." Or do we jab a fork into our friend's fingers and scream, "Mine!" over that little, five-cent potato wedge? That attitude intrudes into the way we look at our other possessions as well. We will spend and spend but give God only the crumbs in our pockets, because it is all ours. It's what I worked all week to earn.

News flash—everything we have is on loan from God. There will be no U-Hauls behind the hearse when we die. Everything we have is God's.

God does not need it, but we want to give back to him as a way of saying thank you! God is good, even when we are not. He does not give us crumbs. He gave his Son, Christ our Savior, who washes away all our sins. That alone makes him good and worthy of our thanks.

- What often gets in the way of us wanting to give God our best?

Pray: Lord, forgive me for being selfish. Help me to give thanks to you in all aspects of my life.

A Good God

❖

He is good.
PSALM 107:1

Context: Psalm 107:1-43

How would you define *good?* Perhaps your definition of good is a fresh pan of Scotcheroo dessert bars. Yes, trust me; they are good. Or maybe you define *good* as a song that you can listen to over and over as you pretend to run on the treadmill. *Good* can also be the high five your boss or teacher gives you after you complete a certain task and do it well.

Like the creamy filling inside a double-stuffed cookie, stuffed between our giving thanks and God's enduring love, we have the psalmist's reminder that God is good. God is perfect and holy. He is a wonderful counselor and a mighty God, and the list goes on and on. And God has our best interests in mind.

Here is a mind-bender too: Even when we are in the midst of struggle and heartache, God is good. Why did he have to die? Why did she have to dump me? Why do I not have many friends? We may not understand it at the time, but we can focus less on the *why* and more on the *who.* God is the One who loves you unconditionally, even enough to send his Son to die for you. He is a God who promises that no matter what happens, he will make all things work—for what? Say it with me: *"Our good."*

Knowing that God has in mind only what is good for us makes him more than good; he's *great!*

- How can we recognize God's goodness in our lives today?

Pray: Lord, thank you for being so good to me, even when I do not recognize it.

An Enduring Love

❖

His love endures forever.

PSALM 107:1

Context: Psalm 107:1-43

"Oh man, I love this song!" Then two weeks pass and another song becomes the sole focus of our love. This can happen not just with songs but also with relationships. Sadly, I have been dumped in the past and can say that, sometimes, love stinks. At least, it really hurts. I remember the thrill of high school romance: long walks to the local ice cream shop to share a turtle sundae—one sundae, two spoons. Ah, love was in the air. Then, only weeks later, my heart was broken by the dreaded "let's be friends" line. Life was brought to a screeching halt as I learned to mend my broken heart. What I thought would last forever was only for a moment, and the moment was gone like dust in the wind.

How about God? Does he love you for what you do for him? Does he love you for your looks, your charm, your smarts? Is his love temporary? No, there is nothing in us to love. If you have endured a broken heart recently, this realization probably doesn't help your broken heart heal. But here is something to focus on: God's love is not a puppy love or an infatuation type of love. His love is rock solid. God does not, nor will he ever, dump you. He doesn't give you the "let's be friends" speech. Instead, he dumped all your sins on his Son, and Jesus made us not "just friends" but God's precious children. You are loved, not just today but forever!

• How is God's love motivating you today?

Pray: God, thank you for always loving me. Help me to be more loving to others.

Ahab and Jezebel

❖

**Ahab . . . did more evil in the eyes of the LORD
than any of those before him. . . . He also married Jezebel
daughter of Ethbaal king of the Sidonians,
and began to serve Baal and worship him.** 1 KINGS 16:30,31

Context: 1 Kings 16:29-33

A fun question to ask high school freshmen is what they would look for in a person they would potentially want to marry. Answers range from someone with a sense of humor to someone who looks like he or she stepped off the cover of a magazine. Understand it is not wrong to be attracted to the appearance of someone you want to date or potentially marry. But what happens after the looks have faded? What is your relationship based on? King Ahab married a Phoenician woman by the name of Jezebel. The problem was that Jezebel brought her false god, Baal, to the relationship. That, in turn, influenced her already evil husband. As a result, the nation of Israel was led even further astray.

To date someone outside of your faith is not wrong per se. Some such relationships have resulted in both people being brought closer to God. But more often than not, we follow Ahab—we end up being led astray. Why? Because we are in love. That type of love is blind—blind to the truth that the only real love is the love the Father lavished on us with his Son's sacrifice. No magazine cover model is worth our soul.

- Relationship questions to ask:
  Will this relationship help me in my relationship
  with God?
  Does this person love me enough to respect and want to
  learn about my beliefs?

Pray: Lord, give me the strength to make the right dating choices.

Elijah on Mount Carmel

❖

The fire of the Lord fell and burned up the sacrifice, the wood, the stones and the soil, and also licked up the water in the trench. . . . The people . . . fell prostrate and cried, "The Lord—he is God!"
1 KINGS 18:38,39

Context: 1 Kings 18:16-39

In 2017, we witnessed the first overtime in Super Bowl history. It was a tale of two halves that featured the epic collapse of one team that had dominated by 20 points and a remarkable comeback by the other team.

However, nothing matches the epic showdown on Mount Carmel. In one end zone were the prophets of the false god Baal. In the other end zone was just one man—Elijah, the prophet of the Lord. Their battlefield was not well-manicured turf but altars. The rules? The prophets who could get their deity to consume the offering with fire would be the winner. The prophets of Baal tried their best Hail Mary plays to get the attention of their god. They even thought if they hurt themselves, their god might listen. But Baal did not respond. Then Elijah dug a trench around his altar and ordered that his altar be soaked with water until the overflow filled the trench. After a simple prayer, fire consumed the altar and everything around it. God proved that he is the true God.

There are times in our lives when we will experience moments of greatness. We can embrace those moments as blessings from God. There will be many times, however, when unbelievers will mock us for our faith. It may even seem like they are winning. Keep in mind that God will not be mocked and that his Word will endure.

Keep fighting the good fight! Know that Jesus has already given us the victory.

- How can God use confrontation with unbelievers as a blessing?

Pray: Lord, give me the courage to stand up for you like Elijah did.

Elijah's Pity Party

❖

**After the earthquake came a fire,
but the LORD was not in the fire.
And after the fire came a gentle whisper.**
1 KINGS 19:12

Context: 1 Kings 19:1-18

Sometimes life just stinks. You oversleep, miss the bus, get to class late, forget there is a quiz in class, get detention. You get the "let's just be friends" speech from yet another potential date, lose your lunch money, strike out in the last inning of the game, get a zit the day before the big dance, get grounded, or lose your phone privileges right after the person of your dreams agrees to actually communicate with you. Oh, the horror! And the list goes on.

Elijah had his Super Bowl moment on Mount Carmel against the prophets of Baal. He proved who the true God is. And his reward? Jezebel put a price on his head, and he ran for his life. He then went on the biggest pity-party trip of his life. He walked into the wilderness and sat down under a bush. "I have had enough, Lord," he said. "Take my life."

How often haven't we taken that trip? What we fail to realize is that, this side of heaven, life will always have its stinky moments. When these moments happen, God reminds us, like he reminded Elijah, that he is still with us. We might not get the big flashy answer to the prayer that we want. But he still assures us through the gentle whisper—his Word—that he is God and he is still in control. As the problems continue in your life, remember that you are not alone. The problems will pass in time. Your God is always with you!

• Where can we hear the still small voice of God today?

Pray: Lord, help me to trust you and to listen for your whisper amidst the chaos of life.

WEEK 24 DAY 3

Elisha's Request

❖

"Let me inherit a double portion of your spirit."
2 KINGS 2:9

Context: 2 Kings 2:9-16

Recently, I met my boyhood idol, William Shatner, who played Captain Kirk on *Star Trek*. I had to stand in a long line and pay a lot. But it was still worth it.

It is amazing what happens when you meet famous people. In your mind, you rehearse the lines you want to say. But when the moment comes, your brain turns to soup. You just stare and awkwardly spit out what you hope sounds like a subject-verb sentence.

Elisha was in the presence of greatness. He knew that Elijah, the Lord's prophet, was going to be leaving him soon. Instead of being tripped up by awe or making a silly request, he asked for a double portion of Elijah's spirit.

In Bible times, a father customarily gave his oldest son a double share of the inheritance. By requesting a double portion of Elijah's spirit, Elisha was asking for that share which belonged to him as Elijah's successor.

If we could ask God for anything, what would we ask for? Money? A date? Or do we follow Elisha's lead and ask God to give us the gifts and the spirit to honor him and benefit God's people?

You do not need to be on TV; you do not need to have people pay for your autograph. That's not what gives value to your life. Jesus, the ultimate celebrity, paid the price to make you his. He signed his name in blood so that his name could be on you. You matter to him. Don't be afraid to ask God to empower you to share that with the next generation.

- God promises to give what we ask for in Jesus' name. What will you ask for?

Pray: Lord, give me the wisdom to ask for and to do what pleases you.

Zechariah's Doubt

❖

**Zechariah asked the angel, "How can I be sure of this?
I am an old man and my wife is well along in years."**
LUKE 1:18
Context: Luke 1:5-20

Your team is under 500 and yet your friend makes the bold prediction that this subpar team will win the championship. You have a major test in the next class; as you pass a friend in the hall, you ask, "What are the odds the teacher will not give us the test?"

In both cases, the response will be, "I doubt that will happen."

The day began like any other uneventful day. Zechariah, the well-seasoned priest, was all set to fulfill his priestly privilege of burning incense in the temple. But something happened that would mark the day for all of history. The angel announced to this elder statesman that he and his wife were going to have a child.

Zechariah's response to the angel in effect said, "I doubt that will happen." But God did keep his promise, and Zechariah and Elizabeth were blessed with a son even in their old age.

When God makes promises to us, how do we react? God says that the struggle you are now having with friends he can work out for good. God says that he will always be with you, even when you struggle with loneliness. The fact that God kept his most important promise, to send his Son to save us from our sins, assures us that God can and will keep every promise that he has made. Our doubts will never negate the promises of God!

- What areas of faith are you struggling with right now?

- What promises do you need to hear over and over again?

Pray: Lord, forgive me for the times I have doubted your promises. Help me to always trust you.

Mary's Trust

❖

No word from God will ever fail.
LUKE 1:37

Context: Luke 1:26-38

My grandmother was a firm believer in the local supermarket tabloid magazines. Headlines would read, "Frog boy—half frog, half boy—leaps to school!" Or, "Elvis is alive and is living on an island with Tupac and Michael Jackson." As you read these articles, you can't help but snicker at their believability. But what about this one: "Virgin gives birth to a child"? Okay, I could already see the cover of the last issue being a big leap: "Aged Elizabeth giving birth to a child." But come on, this "virgin gives birth" one takes the cake. If you know anything about the birds and the bees, this is not the norm. Babies do not come from storks but from God's grand design of a man and woman having sex.

Mary understood this norm, so she asked the angel, "How will this be?"

What follows is one of those what I like to call refrigerator-magnet passages—the kind you hang on the door next to the grocery list and the Christmas cards to remind you daily of a simple truth.

I'm a fan of the older NIV translation that read, "Nothing is impossible with God." We may catch ourselves wondering if there is anything that our God cannot do. Or if we are willing to admit it, we may really think he can't possibly help us in our daily struggles. However, the angel teaches us the simplest of truths: Nothing is impossible for God. Nothing! Nothing! This is not tabloid fodder but biblical truth! We thank God for showing us true faith.

- How does the simple truth that nothing is impossible for God affect the decisions we make today?

Pray: Lord, when I am wrestling with doubts, teach me to trust the angel's words, "NOTHING IS IMPOSSIBLE WITH GOD"!

WEEK 25 DAY 3

Mary's Song

❖

**"My soul glorifies the Lord and
my spirit rejoices in God my Savior."**
LUKE 1:46,47

Context: Luke 1:39-56

What is your favorite song right now? As a child of the 80s, I can think of many of my favorites that have made their way to greatest hits playlists at a few parties. What is it about a song that makes it great? The lyrics? The beat? That booming bass that gets your feet thumping, makes the guys in the next car look twice, or has your parents screaming, "Turn that down!"?

Music is therapeutic and can change your mood. If you do not believe me, try watching a Bugs Bunny cartoon sometime without any music. Without the orchestra, it is very boring. The music adds life and feeling to what is happening on the screen.

I am not sure if Mary's song would make the American Top 40 hit list. However, the song is packed with emotion. Mary sings of her child and how great he will be. She humbly thanks the Lord for the gifts he has given to her and to the world. She also speaks of how the entire world will benefit from this child.

More meaningful than a Grammy, more prestigious than a name on a soundtrack, you have been given the greatest award of all— heaven. Your name is written on the book of life, all because of Mary's child. If music is in your blood, share that gift along with the gift of the Christ Child. Feel like singing yet? I do.

- How big a part does music play in your life?

- How do you use music to glorify God?

Pray: Lord, as I pray, make my heart sing for joy because of your great mercy and the love you have shown to me.

WEEK 26 DAY 1

Jesus Is His Name

❖

**"You will conceive and give birth to a son, and
you are to call him Jesus."**
LUKE 1:31
Context: Luke 1:30-33

Why did your parents give you the name that they did? Perhaps you were named after a biblical character or a relative. I was not named after the gas station or even after Superman's secret identity. My mom is a huge *Gone With the Wind* fan, so I was named after Clark Gable. More than just relying on a sorting hat in a wizarding world, there is much that goes into picking a name. Your parents undoubtedly spent hours thinking of the perfect name for you. But Mary did not have to worry about this. The angel laid it all out for her. His name was to be Jesus, which means "the Lord saves."

Yes, a name can pack a punch. If I were to say the names LeBron, Favre, Mozart, Jobs, or Gates, those names bring images to mind—images of specific people with special gifts. Jesus is the ultimate name. His name alone carries the promise of change and the salvation the world desperately needs.

There is another name we hold on to as well: Christian. This means we are Christ's followers. When people see us, they see Christ. I have to admit that I don't always represent Jesus to others. If you are like me, then focus on the name Jesus. What does that name mean? Say it with me: "You are forgiven. You are saved!"

- List other names for God the Bible gives us. What comfort do you find in those names?

Pray: Jesus, thank you for saving me. May your gift of salvation motivate me to reflect your name to others.

Shepherds

❖

There were shepherds living out in the fields nearby.
LUKE 2:8

Context: Luke 2:8-19

While growing up, I often wondered why God chose the shepherds first to announce his good news. I mean there must have been someone a little more like Paul Revere he could have used to ride through the countryside, shouting, "The Savior is coming! The Savior is coming!" Nope, just some shepherds who smelled like fields and animals and sweat.

What's even more amazing is that once they got the message, they didn't dawdle. They hightailed it to the manger. And even after that, they left the manger all stoked and ready to tell everyone what they had seen. This was a message for all people.

Today, God's message is equally for all people.

As a teen, I never felt like I was in the "in crowd." I played sports, but my usual position on the football team was *left out*. I also hung with the gamers and Sci-Fi group. I was what you would call an in-betweener. I was only sort of a part of either group. If I appreciated anything about this, it is the simple fact that it opened my eyes to the idea that God's message of the Savior is for *all people*. This includes you, me, and everyone else, no matter where they fall on the Cool Meter.

Rejoice with the shepherds that the *Good Shepherd* showed us his manger and uses us to share the good news with others.

- Why doesn't God use angels to announce great news today?

- At times, most of us feel we don't have the gifts to do anything really worthwhile. What's wrong with that thinking?

Pray: Lord, thank you for sharing the good news with me. Give me the courage you gave to the shepherds to share the good news with others.

Angels Sing of Peace

❖

" . . . and on earth peace to those on whom his favor rests."
LUKE 2:14
Context: Luke 2:13,14

An ex-Beatle recorded an anti-war song that had the refrain, "Give peace a chance." Whenever there is a war or crisis, the song and signs bearing this refrain seem to find their way onto the TV screen. The hope of the singers or marchers is that the two warring parties can stop and have peace.

The angels sang to the shepherds about peace. A war had been going on for what seemed like forever. Ever since Adam and Eve fell into sin, we have been at war with God. Even as you read this, the war wages inside of you. You hear a voice that tells you to keep reading, keep feeding your soul, but another voice pipes up: "This is boring; there are more important things you could be doing with your time." To whom do you listen? Some days one voice shouts louder than the other. No earthly treaty can stop the bloodshed. We look to the one who shed his blood to give us peace. His voice, crying out on Calvary's cross, drowns out all the other voices we hear. Yes, give peace a chance—the peace only Christ gives!

- What is the difference between earthly peace and spiritual peace?

- When you don't feel at peace, what can you do?

Pray: Lord, thank you for giving me the peace that surpasses all human understanding.

Mary's Treasure

❖

Mary treasured up all these things and pondered them in her heart. LUKE 2:19

Context: Luke 2:16-19

Somewhere in my parents' attic are all my original *Star Wars* toys. Checking prices on ebay, it seems that these toys, if not chewed up by the mice, are worth some real money. Some would say they are a treasure.

Mary's life had suddenly turned into a roller-coaster ride. Imagine the scenario: one minute you are a typical teenager hanging with your friends; the next you are listening to an angel telling you that you are going to give birth to the Son of God. You are well aware of comments whispered by family and friends, and you see the hurt look on your husband's face as he makes plans to divorce you privately. Then, wait a minute. He believes you now because the angel told him the facts. Next, you need to travel 80 miles (while uncomfortably pregnant) to Bethlehem for a census. Finally, your baby arrives. Angels sing. Shepherds visit. But all of this takes place in a stable, not the Bethlehem Hilton. How would you deal with all of this? Through the good and the bad, Mary didn't complain. Instead, she TREASURED all these moments.

This may be a time in your life when everything is going your way: grades, family, friends, sports. Treasure those moments. On the flip side, maybe you feel like your life is in an animal trough. Even then, treasure these moments. When we experience joys and struggles, we recognize that Jesus was not simply a babe in Bethlehem but is our KING. Earthly toys and toils are temporary. A life with Jesus is for eternity. That is our real treasure.

- What is your number one treasure?

- Why is it so hard to focus on our real treasure of heaven?

Pray: Lord, help me to treasure in my heart both the good and the bad, recognizing that in you all is good.

Anna and Simeon

❖

Simeon took him in his arms and praised God. LUKE 2:28

**[Anna] gave thanks to God and spoke about the child
to all who were looking forward
to the redemption of Jerusalem.** LUKE 2:38

Context: Luke 2:25-38

While I was growing up, I never knew my grandfathers. However, I did have the blessing of knowing both of my grandmothers. They each taught me things like the art of playing cards and board games, who Lawrence Welk was, and top secret family recipes.

It is special now to see the way my parents interact with my children. I once heard a comedian joking about that grandparent/ grandchild relationship: "My children love my mother, and I tell my children, that is not the same woman I grew up with. . . . That is an old woman trying to get into heaven now."

Today we meet two wise veterans of the family of God. Both of them rejoiced in the fact that they were able to live to see this special promise fulfilled. What I like about this reading is what we don't read. Mary and Joseph didn't snatch baby Jesus away from these complete strangers. They didn't run in the other direction. Instead, they let them have their moment with Jesus.

Friends, as we live with and interact with the generation that came before us, remember to pray for them. They may not move as fast as you and they may not be up on all the tech like you are, but they did pave the way for you in the world in which you currently live. And they are special souls for whom Christ died. Show them the love and respect that Mary and Joseph showed, and let them have their moment with Jesus.

- What is one way you can help an elderly person today?

Pray: Lord, give me a heart to view those who are older than I am not as burdens but as people with knowledge and wisdom.

Wise Men

❖

**After Jesus was born in Bethlehem in Judea,
during the time of King Herod,
Magi from the east came to Jerusalem.**
MATTHEW 2:1

Context: Matthew 2:1,2

"Wise men say only fools rush in." Quick, who sang that song? Yes, it was the king of rock and roll: Elvis Presley. Long before rock and roll, some wise men traveled a long distance from the east over some rocky terrain to see the King of kings. While we do not know how many wise men made the journey, tradition has given them names like Caspar, Balthazar, and Melchior. What we do know is this: They did not sit on the promises of God. They read, they came, they saw, and they believed.

These men traveled for months to see Jesus. At times our excuses for not going to church to hear Jesus or for not getting into the Word are real chart toppers: "I am tired." "I worked last night." "I hear about Jesus every day in school; why do I need to go for another hour on Sunday?" And the top ten list of hit reasons goes on and on.

The faith of these wise men carried them through their journey. Their true wisdom was demonstrated by their faith in a promise. The object of their faith, this baby in Bethlehem, did not disappoint. He was the Savior of the world.

A diploma on the wall might tell an onlooker a little about your knowledge. But that diploma will not get you into heaven. A connection with the heavenly King, number one on the charts, gives you the advantage of true wisdom.

• Explain this slogan: "Wise men still seek him."

Pray: Lord, give me the zeal of the wise men to continue to seek the true wisdom that is found in you.

Herod—The Good and the Bad

❖

**When King Herod heard this he was disturbed,
and all Jerusalem with him.**

MATTHEW 2:3

Context: Matthew 2:1-12

I recently ran across a rehab show on TV that told the story of an ex athlete who once had it all: a beautiful wife, money, cars, and the fame that came with a successful basketball career. And yet, here he was on a rehab show. For all he had, there was just one void—the void he felt from the childhood pain of losing his mother. He thought that the only thing that could fill that void was drugs. Later in the show, he admitted that what was really missing in his life was a relationship with God.

King Herod will go down in history as a maniac and a monster. He was a very talented individual and did much to rebuild the temple and restore other buildings in his kingdom. What was missing was a relationship with God. He was so consumed with jealousy that he spent his days killing anyone who threatened his power. This included a wife, three of his sons, a mother-in-law, and her brother. This is why when he heard that a king had been born, "He was disturbed, AND ALL JERUSALEM WITH HIM." They knew what he was capable of doing. The massacre in Bethlehem showed that their fears were legitimate. But his power and possessions didn't last long. And when he died, he couldn't take any of his accomplishments with him.

God blesses us all in different ways! Some will have more or accomplish more than you—others less. The important thing is Christ! His victory over death gives us victory. He is the source of our success, not only in this life but in the next!

- Why was it a blessing that the wise men visited Herod?

Pray: God, give me the resolve to put you first, above everything else in my life.

Wise Men Bring Gifts

❖

They . . . presented him with gifts of gold, frankincense and myrrh.
MATTHEW 2:11

Context: Matthew 2:3-12

What is the best gift you have ever received? I am a fan of creative giving rather than receiving. In a world where many resort to just giving gift cards, the art of gift giving is being lost. It is a joy to give gifts that took some planning and thought. As loved ones open gifts they did not expect, the looks on their faces are priceless.

The wise men brought gifts with significance. They did not just go to Bethlehem's big box store to pick up whatever was on the bargain rack. Instead each gift showed that the wise men knew that this baby was the one foretold in the Scriptures. In those days, who had the most gold or who controlled the gold of the land? Answer: the king. By giving gold, the wise men acknowledged that Jesus is the King of kings. The second gift, frankincense, was used by the priests in the temple and is a fitting gift for Jesus, our true High Priest.

And finally, myrrh is what I like to call "Axe body spray for dead people." One of its many uses was for embalming. This foreshadowed Jesus' humble sacrifice for our sins.

What gifts do we bring to Jesus today? The quick answer is money, and that is correct. But there is more. What unique gifts has God given to you? Music, art, sports, personality? When we use those gifts, we are giving glory to the God who gave us the greatest gift of all.

- What are your special gifts? If you aren't sure, ask a friend what your gifts are.

Pray: Lord, help me not to take the gifts you have given me for granted but rather to use those gifts as a way to worship you.

Jesus in the Temple

❖

**He went down to Nazareth with them and
was obedient to them.**
LUKE 2:51
Context: Luke 2:41-51

As a teen, I didn't always see eye to eye with my parents. We fought about who I hung out with, what clothes I wore, and why I would want to wear my hair the way I did. Some yearbook photos make me wonder the same. My parents were not perfect, and I certainly wasn't.

Now imagine this scene: You are Jesus. You are perfect. Your parents get the award for absentmindedness because they left you behind in Jerusalem.

After three days—yes, three days—they find you in the temple. They scold you. And you respond. Do you let them have it? Do you point out their mistake to everyone in the temple? In the future, whenever you want to gain the advantage in an argument, do you throw this in their faces? Jesus was not about revenge. Instead, he was about doing what was right and doing what his heavenly Father had sent him to do. Though his parents were not perfect, he wanted to honor the Fourth Commandment by showing loving obedience to Mary and Joseph and, in turn, to his heavenly Father.

Perhaps this devotion finds you at odds with your parents. They are not perfect. Like the author of this devotion, neither are you. They are still your parents. Honoring them and giving them respect is not only wise, it shows respect to the One who gave them to you.

- Explain the following sentiment, which is echoed by most adults: "When I was 16 years old, I couldn't believe how clueless my parents were. A few years later, I was surprised by how much they had learned."

Pray: Lord, thank you for giving me parents. Give me also the humility to swallow my pride and to listen to their wise counsel.

Jesus Understands Our Weakness

❖

**The tempter came to him and said,
"If you are the Son of God,
tell these stones to become bread."**
MATTHEW 4:3

Context: Matthew 4:1-4

Superman's weakness is kryptonite. This green meteoric rock from his home planet strips the strongest man of all his power. My personal kryptonite comes in two forms: pizza and chocolate. I have never met a piece of either I did not like. What is your weakness? I am not just talking about food, but I mean for real: what is your weakness? The devil is like an army general who studies us and knows where our weaknesses are and looks to exploit them. Is your weakness a loose tongue? He will put you in areas where gossip is the norm. Is your weakness in the area of sex? He will be sure to put you in situations where the lights are off and parents aren't in sight.

The devil came to Jesus while he was fasting and offered him, of all things, FOOD! After 40 foodless days, Jesus was undoubtedly hungry. But Jesus gave the devil something to chew on, that is, God's Holy Word.

As we go through the devotions this week, it will become easy to get down on yourself as you think of past sins. Don't give the evil general that benefit of the doubt. Remember, though we are weak, Jesus is strong, and because of his strength, we win and are forgiven. Imitate Jesus. Keep God's Word as your sure defense when the evil foe makes his next charge against you!

- In what way was Jesus' temptation similar to the temptation of Adam and Eve? In what ways does Satan come to you with similar temptations?

Pray: Lord, give me the strength to use your Word to fight off the devil.

Jesus Understands When We Do Something Dumb

❖

"If you are the Son of God," he said, "throw yourself down."
MATTHEW 4:6

Context: Matthew 4:5-7

A whole book could be written about the dumb stuff I did in my younger years. Just one example: My brother and I tried to jump our frozen pond with our three-wheelers. The night ended with the two of us lying on the ice with a tow rope and hook, attempting to fish an ATV out of the bottom of the pond.

In our younger years, we often develop a bulletproof mentality. Somehow, we believe that death or other consequences don't apply to us. We drive faster than the speed limit allows. We treat our bodies as if they are our bodies and allow ourselves to do whatever we want with whomever we want, instead of treating our bodies as temples of God.

The devil tried to get Jesus to jump from the peak of the temple. This might seem dumb, but Satan even used Scripture to back up his request: "It is written: 'He will command his angels concerning you, and they will lift you up in their hands, so that you will not strike your foot against a stone'" (v. 6).

Satan likes to twist the Word and take it out of context. Jesus used Scripture to put Satan in his place. While it is true that God's angels do protect us, we are not to put God to the test. Perhaps you are thinking of some dumb things you have said or done, things that have left your heart sunk in a pond. Grab the rope and get up. Jesus defeated Satan with his words and again by rising from the dead. That means we are one hundred percent forgiven.

• What do pride and temptation have in common?

Pray: Lord, strengthen me with your Word to resist the devil and his temptations.

Jesus Gives Us Everything

❖

**"All this I will give you," he said,
"if you will bow down and worship me."**
MATTHEW 4:9

Context: Matthew 4:8-11

Finish the sentence: My life would be so much happier if . . .

The third and final temptation of the devil has always puzzled me. Follow my logic here, and see if you agree.

God created everything, right? That means he owns everything, right? Jesus is God, right? So why does Satan offer Jesus something he already has? It would be like me offering to sell you your own cell phone. It doesn't make sense. But the devil is hoping to trip up Jesus by implying that he has something to offer that God has withheld from Jesus. The devil plays the same game with us today. He tries to get us to think that God is keeping something from us. No one loves me, but I can find love and acceptance in pills, drugs, sexual relationships outside of marriage, or building myself up and tearing others down. But think about it. Did Jesus die on the cross? The answer is yes. Did Jesus die for your sins? The answer is yes. Does this show how much God loves you and that you are loved? The answer is a big time *yes!* So Satan has to adjust his tactic a little: "Then why is it that when you pray to God, his answer is no?"

If God keeps something from us, it is only because he has something better in mind for us!

The devil is great at promising the world up front, but he fails to tell us about the consequences in fine print. With God there is no fine print, just the color of Jesus' blood, which covers your sins.

- What does the fact that Jesus overcame temptation mean for you?

Pray: Jesus, help me to learn that without you I have nothing, but with you I have everything.

Empathetic Jesus

❖

**When the Lord saw her, his heart went out to her
and he said, "Don't cry."**
LUKE 7:13
Context: Luke 7:11-17

The casket is lowered as you say your final goodbye. The final team is posted and your name is not on the list. The person you love betrays you or does not even notice you.

Life sometimes stinks. During those times, friends may try to comfort us but find themselves at a loss for words because they don't really understand. We may throw our hands up and say, "If only someone understood!"

Jesus does.

Jesus saw the scene: The widow had lost her husband and her son. Her means of income was gone. What stared her in the face were empty places at the supper table, the silence of a home that once had been filled with laughter, and almost certain poverty. One sentence from our lesson has always moved me: "His heart went out to her." Jesus, true God but also true man, knew exactly what this woman was feeling. He felt her pain. That is called *empathy*. Now if the story ended there, it would be tragic. But it doesn't. Jesus gave a free ticket to the best reunion concert ever—a mother and son reunited after Jesus raised him from the dead. You who are reading this: God knows what you are going through. What is more, he cares! Whatever it is you are facing, talk to him in prayer. He is listening, and his heart goes out to you!

• What challenge are you facing?

• What will help you remember that Jesus cares?

Pray: Jesus, thank you for knowing what I am feeling. Help me trust you to work everything out for my good.

Caring Mother Equals Persistence

❖

Jesus did not answer a word. So his disciples came to him and urged him, "Send her away, for she keeps crying out after us."
MATTHEW 15:23

Context: Matthew 15:22-28

"Dad, can I have the keys to the car?"

"No, son."

"Dad?"

"Yes, son."

"Can I have the keys to the car?"

"No, son."

"Dad, can I have the keys to the car?"

"No."

"Dad, may I please have the keys to the car?"

"Yes, son!"

While some would say the son here was annoying, others might commend him for his persistence. He knew that if he kept asking, his father would eventually say yes. On the flip side, the father wanted his son to keep asking to teach him not to give up after one try.

In our Bible reading today, we see a woman whose daughter was possessed by a demon. She needed Jesus' help. She kept asking for Jesus' help. Jesus finally responded by stating a reason for not helping her.

The woman didn't give up but kept on asking. Her persistence allowed her request to be answered. When we pray to God, he may answer with no, yes, wait, or "I have something better." When the answer seems to be no, he still wants us to keep asking. He does not want us to give up. He wants us to trust that even if the answer is no, he has something better in mind for us. What he has in mind may be to strengthen our faith. Don't give up; keep asking! Our heavenly Father is listening!

- How many times is too many times to ask God for something?

- What steps could you take to strengthen your prayer life?

Pray: Lord, teach me to have the same kind of faith this woman had and to never give up coming to you in prayer.

Jesus Equals Authority

❖

**They were amazed at his teaching,
because his words had authority.** LUKE 4:32

Context: Luke 4:31-37

Legend has it that in his campaign to conquer the world, Alexander the Great encountered some difficulty when he came to a certain walled city. As Alexander approached the great city, he peered up toward the king who stood on top of the wall and he shouted, "My name is Alexander the Great, and I demand you surrender immediately!"

Laughing, the king asked, "Why should we surrender to you?" He explained that his army outnumbered Alexander's troops and were more than prepared to defend the city.

In response, Alexander turned to his one hundred choice troops and commanded them to line up in perfect order, facing a cliff. Each did so obediently in respect for their leader. Alexander then ordered them to start moving. One by one they began marching toward the edge of the cliff. The first soldier stepped off the cliff and plummeted to his death, as did the second, third, fourth, all the way until the eleventh man.

When Alexander finally yelled, "Halt!" he gazed back at the king who was completely astonished by the obedience and utter respect of the men toward Alexander. The king surrendered immediately, and Alexander went on to conquer the civilized world.

As Jesus began his ministry, the people were amazed at the authority of his words. He quickly showed the extent of his authority. He could command demons to come out of people. Remember that! Jesus' words can send the devil and his cronies packing. Whether we access his words in a printed book or on an app, remember that his Word is our one sure defense against the spiritual enemies we face.

- How does Jesus' authority compare to that of great leaders of history?

Pray: Lord, keep me strong in your Word, which is the ultimate authority over all my foes.

WEEK 31 DAY 1

Friends

❖

**Since they could not get him to Jesus . . . ,
they made an opening in the roof
above Jesus by digging through it
and then lowered the mat the man was lying on.**
MARK 2:4

Context: Mark 2:1-12

A wise teacher once warned me that those whom you hang out with are those whom you can become. He went on to use a more powerful illustration. He said, "Whether you step in cow manure or not, if you are around cow manure long enough, you will smell like you did." His point was simple: if the friends I hang around with are getting in trouble or if I am running with the wrong crowd, I may end up being lumped into that crowd, whether innocent or not. I know what you are thinking, "But am I not to be salt and light to my friends?" Yes, if you have the strength only God can give to be the leader and to stand up to your friends when they are doing wrong.

On the flip side, the guys in our reading for today did everything they could to get their friend to see Jesus. They were denied front door access. Instead of giving up, they went to the roof, cut a hole in it, and lowered their friend through the hole. They did this for one simple reason: to get their friend as close to Jesus as possible. A true friend is someone who will stand by you through everything. Another important identifier is that a true friend is someone who does all that can be done to help and encourage your faith to get closer to Jesus.

- Take the friend inventory, asking which friends get you closer or farther from Jesus.

Pray: Jesus, give me the strength to lead my friends to be closer to you in their faith walks.

WEEK 31 DAY 2

Father Knows Best

❖

"I do believe; help me overcome my unbelief!"
MARK 9:24

Context: Mark 9:14–27

It is easy to see and to say that God loves you when skies are blue. How about when dark clouds hit? When you lose a job, lose a friend, get dumped, fail a test, get cut from the team, or . . . ? Do I need to go on? Does God still love you then?

Of course he does. He allows these struggles to touch our lives in order to steer us closer to his Word and to remind us that he is in control. However, this is where the spiritual tennis match gets played—God on one side, the devil on the other. The devil will serve up some good lies to get you to cheer for his team. "God doesn't love you if he allows this to happen in your life." Or, "If God really cared, he would give you this." All lies. Out of bounds spiritually.

The man we read about above had a son who was demon possessed. Jesus came to the father and invited him to trust that he could help him. The father's response puts into words something that we all struggle with daily. Simply put, it is an admission: Yes, God, I know that you are in control and that you love me, but I doubt it too.

To combat this, we need to realize a simple truth: faith either grows or it dies. The more we stay plugged in to God and his Word, the stronger our faith will be and the more we will be able to see through the storms of life to recognize the blue skies God has up ahead.

- What doubts do you have about God and his love for you?

- What opportunities are there to strengthen your faith?

Pray: I do believe; help me overcome my unbelief.

Devil Equals Smoke and Mirrors

❖

Jesus turned and said to Peter, "Get behind me, Satan! You are a stumbling block to me; you do not have in mind the concerns of God, but merely human concerns." MATTHEW 16:23

Context: Matthew 16:21-27

You rewind it over and over, but you still can't see how the magician did that trick.

The devil has been using the same bag of tricks since the fall into sin. When he rebelled against God, his next trick was to take down God's prized creation.

In Jesus' day, the devil perhaps seemed more blatant in his attempts to knock Jesus off the course of being our Savior. In the verse above, we see how he even used a well-intentioned disciple to try to stop Jesus.

Today he generally uses a more subtle approach. He does not need the whole red pitchfork and cape outfit when he can use more smoke and mirrors to get us. Answer a few questions below:

Does the video game you play honor God and the life he created?

Does the magazine you read glorify self-image instead of the renewed image of Christ within us?

Does the television show you watch glorify violence or alternative living?

Do the movies you watch promote premarital sexual activity and drug use?

Do the songs you listen to use foul language to make a point?

Do your point-and-clicks take you to dark places?

If you answer yes or "I don't know" to any of these questions, beware of being duped by the devil. Wake up and stop buying into his lies.

The devil is a caged lion. A caged lion can't hurt you if you don't get close. However, if you start tiptoeing near the cage, watch out!

• What steps can we take to avoid being duped by the devil?

Pray: Lord, open my eyes to see to the devil's tricks.

The Disciples

❖

"Put your sword back in its place," Jesus said to him, "for all who draw the sword will die by the sword." MATTHEW 26:52

Context: Matthew 26:45-54

Local law enforcement spoke to our school about what we should do in the event of an active shooter incident: Run to the nearest exit. If there is no exit, find the safest place to hide. If those first two options fail, fight.

Long before there were active shooters, Jesus' ragtag group of disciples demonstrated the safety procedures outlined by the police officers: run-hide-fight.

When Judas and the temple guards came to Gethsemane to ambush Jesus, the rest of the disciples reacted in a variety of ways. Some showed their true colors and ran. Some went into hiding. Peter, thinking perhaps it was time for the return of David, reached for his sword and lopped off an ear.

Sure, it was dark. Sure, it was a scary situation. But didn't their three years with Jesus teach them anything?

How about you? When you are backed into a corner or surrounded by those who clearly hate you for your faith, how do you react? Run, hide, or fight? Jesus reminded his disciples that those who live by the sword will die by the sword. He asks us to love our neighbors as ourselves. Jesus also encourages us to be bold when it comes to our faith and our witness. What was happening that night in Gethsemane was the unfolding of the greatest story ever told: God's plan to redeem humankind from the power of sin and death. In the battle against Satan's evil, there is a better strategy: proclaim. Tell others what Jesus has done.

- In what ways does the world sometimes ambush you?

- How can you make sure you are prepared for an ambush?

Pray: Encourage me, Lord, to be bold and to not hide my faith.

Peter Disowns Jesus

❖

"Before the rooster crows, you will disown me three times."
MATTHEW 26:75
Context: Matthew 26:31–35,69–75

The phrase "talking out of both sides of his mouth" is used to describe someone whose words can't be trusted. Do you know anyone like that? In one breath they will say they love tacos, but to the next person, they will say that they loathe tacos. Which is it?

Peter was no different. In front of his peers in the upper room, he had boldly confessed, "I will never fall away from you." Then fast forward a few hours. Peter and John get a backdoor pass to Jesus' trial. Here bold Peter is taken down by a lowly servant girl. She confronts Peter. What does Mr. Bold do? He denies he even knows Jesus, and not once but three times. He embellishes his point with a few curses to show how tough he is. Then the rooster crows and he is brought back to reality. He messed up.

But before you are too hard on Peter, remember how often we are like him. We stood at the confirmation altar and promised to love God till the end. But when we are confronted with who we are or who we serve, we fold. We cave to the peer pressure and say, "Jesus who?" But look at Peter. The difference between Peter and Judas in this case is dramatic. They both denied Jesus, but Peter ran to Jesus and was forgiven. Judas did not. When you mess up—and, yes, you will—remember to run to Jesus and let his forgiveness wrap its arms around you!

- How do you deny Jesus?

- How can you be better prepared to be bold for Christ?

Pray: Jesus, when I'm confronted, help me to stand up for you. Forgive me for the times I have not.

WEEK 32 DAY 3

Judas

❖

**Judas threw the money into the temple and left.
Then he went away and hanged himself.** MATTHEW 27:5

Context: Matthew 27:1-5

Two friends each attempted suicide. The first, distraught because of a relationship breakup, decided to "show them" and died of a self-inflicted gunshot wound. What did that accomplish? Yes, it caused sadness. But the former significant other eventually married and raised a family. The parents of the deceased were the ones who carried the deepest scars.

The other friend had been the class president—well-respected by his classmates, teachers, and his parents. When he sinned sexually and his girlfriend became pregnant, he didn't think he could bear the shame and embarrassment, so he took a knife and cut his wrists. By God's grace, the cuts were in the wrong direction. With immediate medical attention, he survived. And by the grace of God, he repented and was assured that his sin was forgiven.

Judas, like Peter, messed up. When he sold out his best friend for chump change, the devil knew how to exploit his weakness. Thinking that his sin was too great, Judas took his own life.

We mess up. Perhaps we sin sexually or betray the trust of a friend. The devil loves to play mind tennis with us. "How could God forgive me?" The devil tempts us to think our situation is hopeless.

Suicide is a permanent solution to a temporary problem. It is a misguided and unfortunate solution. Peter messed up royally, but Jesus forgave him and reinstated him. And Peter became one of the greatest apostles in the New Testament church. No sin is too great for God to forgive. You are forgiven; you are loved; God has great plans for you.

- Who do you know who needs to be reminded of God's forgiveness?

Pray: Lord, I am sorry, but I know you forgive and love me. Please remind me of this daily.

96

Disciples—Before and After

❖

**On the evening of that first day of the week,
when the disciples were together, with the doors locked
for fear of the Jewish leaders . . .** JOHN 20:19

**All of them were filled with the Holy Spirit and
began to speak in other tongues.** ACTS 2:4

Context: John 20:19,20; Acts 2:1-4

Makeover shows are a popular craze on TV these days. The shows cover the gamut from weight loss, to hair and wardrobe, to my favorite—the home makeover. One home makeover show, at the conclusion of every episode, has the family standing in front of a bus blocking the view of their made-over home. The big reveal comes as the bus pulls away and the family is shown what their new home looks like. The expressions say it all.

During the morning on the day of Pentecost, the disciples received a makeover as well. At first, they were pretty quiet. They had locked themselves away in their homes. They were afraid and still had no clue what to do or say.

Enter the Holy Spirit. He gave the disciples the makeover they needed. He encouraged them with the Word and his presence. Now, instead of fear, they had courage to stand up for Christ.

The Holy Spirit works the same way today. As we dig into God's Word, study it, and apply it to our lives, a change takes place. Our fears shrink, and our faith grows! Once our faith grows, we can't help speaking about what we have seen and heard.

- Agree or disagree: We have opportunities to witness for Jesus every day.

- How can you prepare yourself so that you are ready to make use of those opportunities?

Pray: Lord, thank you for giving me a spiritual makeover by taking away my sins and making me alive through faith.

Paul Follows Jesus

❖

**Is Christ divided? Was Paul crucified for you?
Were you baptized in the name of Paul?
I thank God that I did not baptize any of you
except Crispus and Gaius, so no one can say
that you were baptized in my name.**

1 CORINTHIANS 1:13-15

Context: 1 Corinthians 1:10-17

The athlete makes the shot. His immediate reaction is to pound his chest and then look into the camera and go on a rant about how great he and his team are.

One can take a tip of humility from the apostle Paul. Instead of letting the Corinthians know how lucky they were to have him as their apostle, he pointed them to Christ. He let them know that Christ is where their focus should be. Christ is not divided. Christ is the one who gave his undivided life for them. Paul didn't.

Paul exemplifies what we want in a leader—someone who is humble and gives credit where credit is due. Paul was one of the greatest apostles of the New Testament. He didn't point to himself but to the one who gave himself to make us great! Jesus, how great thou art! We say thank you for making us your own.

When you do something well, don't pound your chest. Look to the one who allowed others to pound nails into his hands to make you *great!*

- Why is it hard to be humble?

Pray: Lord, help me to give you praise and credit in all circumstances.

Paul Undivided

❖

I appeal to you . . . that there be no divisions among you.
1 CORINTHIANS 1:10

Context: 1 Corinthians 1:10-15

I love all-you-can-eat buffets. Grab a plate, load up on break-fast items, and chow down. Then go back (taking a clean plate, of course) and get fried chicken, potatoes, pizza, and corn. When that is done and there's "some" room left, hit the dessert bar for some chocolatey goodness. It's fun to have options to choose from.

Sometimes this thinking trickles into the church. We want to make church into a smorgasbord. We may pick favorites when it comes to the man in the pulpit and may even consider skipping church if pastor so-and-so is preaching.

The people of Corinth were no different. This port city was much like New York City. It was a sophisticated city, blessed with commerce of every kind and a variety of cultures reflecting many ethnicities. It also was dripping with false teachings. The church of Corinth was not immune to these teachings. Twice Paul wrote to this congregation to steer the ship back to the port of the Word.

In the context of this particular lesson, we see that factions were forming within the church. Some didn't want to listen to Paul, so they claimed to follow Apollos. The Peter, or Cephas, crowd went their own way as well. Still others made the pious-sounding claim that they didn't need to listen to anyone but Christ.

God has placed called servants in his church. They all have different gifts. Still, they are Christ's representatives. Instead of looking for ways to tear them down, let's look for ways to be united, to follow them, and to encourage them in their ministries.

- How does Satan try to ruin a good thing in the church?

Pray: Lord, teach me to put human pride aside and to follow you and those who care for my soul.

A Wise Paul

❖

**Christ did not send me to baptize,
but to preach the gospel—
not with wisdom and eloquence,
lest the cross of Christ
be emptied of its power.**
1 CORINTHIANS 1:17

Context: 1 Corinthians 1:17-25

K.I.S.S. is an acronym for Keep It Simple Stupid. Things tend to work best if they are kept simple rather than made more complicated. This truth can be applied to a project for class. When you present to a class, the teacher doesn't want to see 18 different fonts and 19 pictures on one slide. Keep it simple and basic and people will be able to follow it much more easily.

Paul followed that principle when he presented the message of Jesus to the Corinthians. The Greek word for "wisdom" is found 51 times in the entire New Testament, yet it appears 16 times in the first chapters of 1 Corinthians alone. The people of Corinth took pride in their wisdom. True, there were some smart cookies living there. But their brand of wisdom did not help them. And as it was then, so it is now: The smarter we get, the less we think we need God—we think we can figure out all of life's problems on our own. This wisdom is not simple. Rather, it complicates issues. Human wisdom cannot, nor will it ever be able to, save you. The cross of Christ is emptied of its power when too much is made of human wisdom and eloquence. If you want to keep it simple, put human wisdom in the back seat and simply preach Christ crucified.

- How does wisdom get in the way of the cross?

Pray: Lord, teach me to make your cross my main source of wisdom.

God's Time

❖

With the Lord a day is like a thousand years, and a thousand years are like a day.

2 PETER 3:8

Context: 2 Peter 3:3-9

Have TV streaming services saved or ruined the experience of watching TV? While some argue it has ruined TV, I believe differently. We live in a society of instant gratification. We expect our overpriced coffee in seconds. We are tapping the steering wheel if the fast-food worker doesn't get our "healthy" burger to us within two minutes from the time we placed our order. A local law firm is currently airing a commercial that has customers yelling at the camera, "It's my money, and I want it right now!"

The funny thing is, God's timetable and our timetables are on different clocks. The world will tell you: *Get it now. Why wait until marriage to have sex? Are you getting good grades? If not, why not cheat? You should expect to make the team and to play on a winning team with zero effort in the off season. It's your right. You should want it right now.*

Think again. God's timetable is different. We can learn a lesson from streaming services. Most streaming services release their shows a year after they have been out, as they get ready for the new season. So if you are patient, you can watch all 13-plus episodes of your favorite show at once. It is worth the wait! No more cliff-hangers! Patience pays off.

God asks us to be patient with him. Deny the instant gratification the world tells you that you deserve. Wait on his promises because he has a much better season in heaven waiting for you!

- At what times do you find yourself the most impatient?

Pray: Lord, forgive my impatience, and teach me that waiting on your promises is always for my good.

The Lord's Day

❖

The day of the Lord will come like a thief.

2 PETER 3:10

Context: 2 Peter 3:10-13

One of my friends was robbed. The robbery took place the night before his wedding. He had just finished his seminary vicar year, so his car was packed with all his belongings. We met him at a local pub in Milwaukee to toast his last night of being single. When we walked to his car an hour later, we noticed the telltale glass on the ground by his front passenger window. Aside from a few CDs, it appeared that most of his belongings were there. Then he noticed that his briefcase was missing in action—the briefcase that contained their marriage license, their passports, and their wedding rings.

When someone steals something from you, you feel so vulnerable. And now we even have to be on guard against cyber crimes and identity theft. What can we do to prevent such crimes? Be more vigilant and watchful! Because most robberies take place in the dark or when no one is watching, we understand why the Bible compares the last days to a thief in the night. God encourages us to be ready—to be vigilant in this dark world. Not just to have our cars or personal information locked up but to have our hearts in tune with God and the security his Word provides. His Word is that light and lamp for us in these dark days of this world. It is also the only protection we need and the best assurance we have!

- What steps can you take to be ready for the Last Day?

Pray: Lord, equip me with the armor of your Word to be ready for the day when you come again.

A Reminder From Peter

❖

"God does not show favoritism."
ACTS 10:34

Context: Acts 10:9-35

"Mom always liked you best!" "Teacher's pet!" "Why does the coach always play them more than me when I am clearly the better player?" From the playground to the real world, we have either uttered, thought, or lived these words. Why them and not us?

Our sinful natures like to play with our minds to make us think that we have been shorted and that we deserve more. But here's a few things to keep in mind: First, we all deserve hell. Second, God doesn't give us what we deserve, but he punished his Son for us. If we can all agree on those two things, then the next few lines will put things into perspective. God does not show favoritism. Whether you are blessed with athletic ability or musical skill, whether you are good with your hands or still trying to figure out what you're good at, you are one hundred percent loved by God! There is no teacher's pet or playing time issues with God because we are all equally his children. Race, gender, bank account, beauty—doesn't matter. There is no segregation. Yes, some may have different gifts and talents than you do. However, that does not take away from the fact that the Creator of the universe created and loves you dearly.

- What makes you feel inferior or jealous of others?

Pray: God, thank you for treating me like your dearly loved child. Remind me that you never pick favorites but love me and others the same.

Jesus Fixes Us Up

❖

**. . . fixing our eyes on Jesus,
the pioneer and perfecter of faith.**
HEBREWS 12:2

Context: Hebrews 12:1-3

Another take on the home makeover theme is a show that focuses on the transformation of old, beat-up homes that the owners buy with the goal of fixing them up. The conclusion is always worth the wait. As the homeowners stand in front of a huge picture of the old run-down home, the show hosts ask their trademark question, "Ya'll ready to see your fixer upper?" As the picture halves slide away, the homeowners experience firsthand the meaning of the phrase "out with the old and in with the new." And all in the blink of an eye.

At the first Pentecost, we witness a similar scene. As the Holy Spirit descends on these disciples, the timid fishermen disappear. In their places, bold witnesses are ready to die for their Savior.

They truly were fixed up! So are you!

There are days we feel broken, tired, or weary from the daily grind of life. The Holy Spirit comes to us in his Word and encourages us to "[fix] our eyes on Jesus." Jesus is the one who makes the difference in our lives. His work and his forgiveness give our lives a completely new look.

Life will not always be easy! But when we slide away the blinders, we are able to take in the sight of a very different type of craftsmanship—a wooden cross. And you are in that picture—no longer broken but a dearly loved, forgiven, special creation of God!

- If we are fixed up spiritually, why do we so often still feel down?

Pray: Lord, thank you for fixing me up!

Peter's Sermon

❖

**Peter replied, "Repent and be baptized,
every one of you,
in the name of Jesus Christ
for the forgiveness of your sins."** ACTS 2:38

Context: Acts 2:22-41

What makes a sermon great? My students enjoy giving a tongue-in-cheek answer like, "It needs to be short." Once those token answers are out of the way, the students give some amazing, insightful answers. "The sermon needs to apply to my life." "It should have a theme and parts." And the granddaddy of them all: "It should contain law and gospel."

A seminary professor once told our class that every sermon needs both law and gospel, just as every plane needs two wings. You can only get so far on an airplane with one wing. Yet today some churches eliminate the law. They want to give you the feel-good fuzzies. But when they do that, they water down the gospel. Why would anyone recognize their need for a Savior if the law hasn't been given the opportunity to do its work? The reverse is also true if the preacher goes all fire and brimstone and leaves out the gospel. That leaves the hearer feeling helpless and hopeless. Many people have been turned off to church by a gospel-less message.

Peter's sermon was excellent. He showed the people their sins: they had crucified the Messiah. But when they expressed sincere repentance, he clearly offered the sweet news of forgiveness.

We need to be hit over the head with the 2 x 4 of God's law to crush our old Adam and lead us to repentance. And then we receive the sweet medicine of forgiveness that gives us a new lease on life.

- Pick out the law and the gospel in the next sermon you hear.

Pray: Lord, thank you for showing me my sins with the law and for showing me my Savior with the gospel.

Jerusalem Christians Share

❖

All the believers . . . shared everything they had.
ACTS 4:32

Context: Acts 4:32-35

You and your friend both order number 1 on the menu (super-sized, of course). You go grab your diet soda. (Surely that will cancel out the 1,400 calories sitting on your tray.) You sit down, say a prayer, and look up just as your friend across the table is grabbing one of your fries. What is your immediate reaction? Is it to stab him with your spork and yell, "MINE"? And this over an eight cent french fry? Or do you look at him and say, "Dude, what's mine is yours"?

The early Christian church had that latter mentality when it came to their possessions. They were not hoarding possessions for themselves, but they shared with those in need. What motivated them to do this? They knew that everything they had was on loan from God. God gave them all of their blessings.

God has blessed you in many ways. Understand that God is not telling you to sell everything and live in a cardboard box. But perhaps this passage encourages you to think about all that you have. Maybe you could look at your wardrobe to see if there is something you do not wear much or something you could donate. Or consider your paycheck. Could you buy one less video game and then give some money to help your local pregnancy counseling center?

Your motivation for doing this is not that some random pastor is laying a guilt trip on you. Your motivation is always and only Christ, who gave ALL of himself completely for you! That's what motivated the first church. May that be our sole motivation today.

- What do you have that you could share with someone in need?

Pray: Lord, teach me to be less focused on me and more focused on your love. Let that motivate me to share with others.

Ananias and Sapphira

❖

"Ananias, how is it that Satan has so filled your heart that you have lied to the Holy Spirit?"

ACTS 5:3

Context: Acts 4:32–37; 5:1–11

My date with the cute waitress was all set—dinner and a movie. A few hours before the big event, a friend called. His girlfriend had just dumped him, and he wanted me to come over. Hmmm. What to do? I called the cute waitress, and I lied. I told her I was sick and could not go out. She understood. My brokenhearted friend said he needed to get out of the house and wanted to go see a movie. As the movie was about to begin, a hand pushed me from behind and I heard a familiar voice say, "Too sick to go out, huh?" Yes, you guessed it; it was the waitress, who now looked more angry than cute. Needless to say, I did not enjoy the movie, and the shouting match in the parking lot afterwards resembled an episode of the TV show *Cops*. I lied. I got busted. Moral of the story: I should have told the truth. And not just because I got busted. The devil is the father of lies. I dishonored God by telling that lie.

Ananias and Sapphira thought that lying was a little thing. They thought that they were simply pulling the wool over the eyes of some of their compatriots in the early Christian church. They were more concerned about being honored as generous donors to the congregation than about honoring God by telling the truth. We all learn an important lesson here. God is serious when he asks us to keep his commandments. White lies or cover-ups do not get rid of sin. Only the blood of Jesus cleanses us.

- Why is it easier to lie than to tell the truth?

Pray: Lord, teach me to trust you and to be honest with others.

Jerusalem Church Worship

❖

They devoted themselves to the apostles' teaching and to fellowship, to the breaking of bread and to prayer.
ACTS 2:42

Context: Acts 2:1–47

When the word *church* is mentioned, what thoughts come to mind? The building, the people, the sound of singing?

Four things stood out as identifying features of the early Christian church: the apostles' teaching—God's Word, fellowship—being one in faith, the breaking of bread—the Lord's Supper, and prayer—mutual prayer. The word *devoted* means that they concentrated their time and energy on these four things.

A sports fan who is devoted to his team is not afraid to show his team's colors. In a similar way, Christians are determined to make these features the priority of our worship life. If you are still reading this book—obviously you are—you have devoted yourself to these things. This *devotion* is what helps focus your attention on your relationship with God.

Perhaps there have been times when we have neglected church, thinking that there are more important things we should be doing. This attitude gives us the stigma of being more like fair-weather fans and not devoted fans.

One of the great blessings of being together with fellow Christians is that we can encourage one another. We are in a room full of fellow sinners who are redeemed just as we are.

Have you heard people talk about strength in numbers? That is the feeling we have in church.

Another way to look at it is that the church is a hospital for sinners and not a hotel for saints. There is always room for one more!

• Who could you invite to church this Sunday for worship?

Pray: Father, help me to be devoted in my worship of you.

Jerusalem Church Having Fun

❖

Every day they continued to meet together. . . . They broke bread in their homes and ate together with glad and sincere hearts, praising God and enjoying the favor of all the people. And the Lord added to their number daily.
ACTS 2:46,47

Context: Acts 2:41-47

How do you react when you hear that the members of the early Christian church gave their stuff away—that they shared all they had with one another? "Thanks but no thanks"? "I need to have a little fun in life too"? What if I told you that you can have your cake and eat it too?

Scripture tells us that they ate together and enjoyed one another's company—they had fun hanging out with one another. This changed the stigma of *church* for the people outside the church. Instead of viewing church just as a place of rules—of dos and don'ts—they recognized that the church was made up of real people, like you and me, who worshiped but also enjoyed the blessings of life.

We might be quick to say, "But my church is anything but fun." And Satan might get us to use that as an excuse for not going to church. I give you this challenge: What are you doing to change the perspective? Complaining about what your church does not have will not bring about change. Only the gospel does that. Use the gospel and the gifts God has given you to make a difference in your church. Maybe there are others in your church who are yearning for connections with other believers. You are the church now! With the Spirit's help, grab some cake, grab some friends, and go have fun this Sunday at church!

- What events at your church could you become more involved in?

Pray: Lord, help me to view the church not as a negative but as a positive place where my faith can grow and I can have fun with other believers.

Unentitled

❖

**Since everything will be destroyed in this way,
what kind of people ought you to be?
You ought to live holy and godly lives.**
2 PETER 3:11

Context: 2 Peter 3:10-12a

After his team's third consecutive loss, a college coach ranted during a postgame interview that we are raising a generation of children who feel entitled and expect everything for nothing. His point was that in order to learn valuable life lessons, the next generation needs to understand that there will be winners and losers. No one is just going to hand you a win (or a job) because you are you. Rather, be faithful and diligent and respect the work of those who have gone before you.

Sadly, the feeling of entitlement has wormed its way into the spiritual realm. If, on judgment day, God asks you why you should be allowed into heaven, what will you say? I'm entitled to it? I deserve it? Do we feel God is being unfair when he says he will punish sins with eternal hellfire? Friends, there will be no consolation prize on judgment day. The two options for our final destination are heaven or hell. Our good works will not earn us any spot on God's team. When we take a serious look at our sins, we see how unentitled we are to be with God forever. We acknowledge the reality and repent.

How, then, do we get on the winning team? We do nothing; it has all been done for us! Jesus laid down his life to pay the price that secured our spots in heaven. The price—his blood. Heaven is ours by grace alone. So what does that motivate us to do? Peter tells us, "You ought to live holy and godly lives."

- What brings about feelings of entitlement?

Pray: Jesus, help me to live in a way that demonstrates my understanding that all I have is from you.

110

Impactful

❖

**Since everything will be destroyed in this way,
what kind of people ought you to be?
You ought to live holy and godly lives.**
2 PETER 3:11

Context: 2 Peter 3:11-14

What is the only thing you can take to heaven with you? Answer: people. What does that say about the way we should live our lives on a daily basis? Yes, we need money and food and the essentials to survive. However, have those become our focus and our god? Almost every year after the holiday and special Black Friday shopping sprees, we see video of a fight that broke out at a big box store. Over what? A doll that talks? A piece of tech that will be outdated in three months? A wise seminary professor once told us, "Gentlemen, look around your home and take an inventory. The golf clubs, the boats, the big screens, the racks of clothes, and the fridge full of food will all be charcoal on the Last Day." The only thing left standing will be people. So what does that say about how you live your life? I remember another quote: "What you have is a gift from God. How you use that gift is your gift back to God." Friends, the talents and the blessings you have are not evil. Putting them in the trophy case of your heart is. Use the gifts and talents that God has given you to make a lasting impression on the world and an impression for the world to come.

- Where can you make an impact today?

Pray: Lord, lead me to cherish each day of your grace and to live each day for you.

Hardships

❖

**"We must go through many hardships
to enter the kingdom of God."**
ACTS 14:22

Context: Acts 14:8-22

I will give you everything in my wallet (which I believe is currently $3.00, a Subway gift card with $1.37 left on it, and a punched
milk card) if you can show me in the Bible where it says that you
will never face troubles in your life. Okay, go on. I'll wait. . . .
Didn't find anything, did you? Nowhere in Scripture does it say
that because you have been baptized, go to church, perhaps even go
to a Christian school, you will not have bad days. On the contrary,
the Bible assures us that we will have hardships.

And not just some but *many* hardships.

As Paul and Barnabas made their way home at the end of their
first missionary journey, they could recount many of the hardships
they had endured: jealousy, hatred, and stoning. And they knew
there would be many more. However, they did not focus on that.
Instead, they focused on the positives. God's Word had reached
places it had never been heard before.

When we face troubles (yes, they will come), are we glass-half-
empty people or glass-half-full people? Instead of focusing on
the hardships, focus on God and his promises. You've heard the
statement, "When life gives you lemons, make lemonade." Think
about that when hardships come. Focus on the God who loves you,
blesses you, and promises to work in all, even the hardships, for
your good. And enjoy the lemonade!

• How can hardships result in stronger faith?

Pray: Help me trust you in all the circumstances of my life, Lord,
even if I do not understand why things happen the way they do.

A Chosen People

❖

You are a chosen people.

1 PETER 2:9

Context: 1 Peter 2:4-9

In grade school, was anything better than lunchtime recess? Remember the rousing games of four square, kickball, and hoops? What was dreaded, though, were the moments leading up to a game. Everyone lined up against the fence while the captains eyed you up to see who they would pick. Name after name would be called. Finally, after what seemed like an eternity, your name was called. As you walked to join your new teammates, your heart was pounding and there was a skip in your step—because you were chosen.

As a believer, that feeling is much the same. Because we are sinful human beings, we like to think that we are the captains of our own lives. We like to play the game of life by our own rules—rules that end up getting us kicked off the team. God has every right to pass us by or, even worse, to let us hang out on the fences of hell. Instead, God comes to us. He seeks us out with his Word. Despite our sin, HE PICKS US!

Whether or not sports is your thing, you are part of a team—God's team. By God's grace through Christ, you belong on the winning team. You have permission to start smiling and skipping now!

- How does the fact that you have been picked by God affect the choices you make?

Pray: Lord, of all the billions of people, you have chosen me. Thank you for your grace.

A *Royal* Priesthood

❖

You are . . . a royal priesthood.
1 PETER 2:9

Context: 1 Peter 2:9,10

Back in 2011, my wife and thousands of other women across the globe were glued to their screens watching a royal wedding. A few years later, the birth of the newest prince stirred up the same fires of infatuation. Face it. People are obsessed with royalty. One wonders if this obsession grows out of fantasy. Many girls dream of being a princess and someday marrying a prince. But then the screen goes dark and reality sets in. We realize that our family lives are less like a fairy tale and more like a nightmare.

Friends, you can have your royal cake and eat it too. You are royalty. No need to do a double take and look for your crown. Jesus our Savior will give us an all-expenses paid trip to the palace of heaven. What is more, God has adopted you into his family. You are his dear child.

For some of you, it may seem that you have the best family in the world. For others, it may seem like the love in your family has taken a commercial break. In either case, you can be sure that God has made you a part of his special family. You are priceless to him— enough to die for. You have the crown of life, and you are part of the best family ever—God's. You are princesses and princes. You are royalty!

- What is the difference between an earthly crown and a heavenly crown?

- When we are feeling down, what can we do to help us remember who we really are?

Pray: Lord, thank you for making me part of your royal family.

A Royal *Priesthood*

❖

You are . . . a royal priesthood.
1 PETER 2:9

Context: 1 Peter 2:9,10

How long did it take you to get up the courage to ask your parents for the keys to the car? Or if you wanted to go a friend's house for the weekend, did you stare in the mirror, repeating the question over and over and listing all the reasons and rationalizations for your request? When the big moment came, did you cautiously walk in and take three deep breaths before asking your parents for permission and then awaiting their answer? All this for one request!

In the Old Testament, God gave the priests a special function that no one else possessed. They could offer sacrifices. Animal after animal, day after day. To remind them of the seriousness of their sins and that their sins separated them from God, the rest of the people weren't allowed to offer sacrifices.

Once Jesus' sacrifice was complete, the veil of the temple tore into two pieces. We can now approach God with confidence and not out of fear. Anytime! Anywhere! We can come to God with our prayers.

God gives us more than the keys to the car; he gives us the keys to heaven. This is his gift to you!

- How does a Christian today make sacrifices to God?

Pray: Lord, thank you for giving me the confidence to approach you in prayer. Give me the confidence also to know that whatever the answer may be, you always have my best interests in mind.

Dark to Light

❖

**You are . . . a holy nation . . . that you may declare
the praises of him who called you out of darkness
into his wonderful light.**
1 PETER 2:9

Context: 1 Peter 2:4-10

A famous movie series depicts the struggle of the main character to resist turning to the dark side. Since episodes 1-3 in the movie series are over 10 years old, I assume I am not giving away any spoilers when I say that the main character gives in and does become evil. Only later in episodes 4-6 of the series does his son rescue him and bring him back to the good side.

We know what it is like to face a daily struggle. We know what God wants us to do, but we struggle internally because the sinful nature within us wants us to do what is evil. God rescued us from the dark side and has brought us into his family. It is through faith in Jesus alone that we are holy. When God sees us, he sees us washed clean by the blood of his Son! Being children of the light, our life takes on a different meaning and purpose. Peter tells us that because we have been rescued from the dark side, we can share the light of Christ with others. I know we can come up with excuses about why we can't or why we are not qualified to share the light of Christ. But we are! We are qualified because Christ made us holy! Yes, the struggle will still go on for us every day. But keep connected to Christ and his Word. He has already won the battle for us.

- What sins most tempt you to the dark side?

Pray: Jesus, thank you for making me holy! Continue to give me the strength to walk with you in the light.

You Belong to God

❖

You are . . . God's special possession.
1 PETER 2:9

Context: 1 Peter 2:9,10

A popular children's animated movie series depicts toys coming to life. In the initial movie, the toys were on a mission to be reunited with their owner. One of the two main characters, a toy cowboy, had the name of his owner, Andy, written on the bottom of his boot (the same boot that had a snake in it). This toy's sole allegiance was to his owner. He belonged to Andy as a prized possession and would do anything to be with him.

How do you view God? Is he the God of doom and gloom? From the Bible, we know he isn't. Is he the God we run from when troubles come? From experience, we know we don't. Let's look at the other side of the coin. How does God view you?

Friends, you are God's prized creation. You are not some random person who is here on this earth by chance. You are special to God. He died for you. You are not God's slaves but his sons and daughters. God does not toy with you but works all circumstances out for your good. Say it with me: "I matter. I am special to God." Yes, you are, and your name is written in the book of life!

• How does being special to God affect your attitude?

Pray: Dear God, thank you for making me yours. During those times when I feel left out and alone, give me the confidence and the assurance that I am and will always be special to you!

Timothy Is Plugged In

❖

As for you, continue in what you have learned.
2 TIMOTHY 3:14

Context: 2 Timothy 3:10-14

One morning when I was coming back from the local dump, I detected a certain odor coming from under the hood of my father's 1985 Ford Ranger. My natural reaction was to do what anyone with uncommon sense would do—speed up and try to get home faster. The result was that the engine overheated and I was forced to pull over to the side of the road. I made a quick call to my wife, and then it happened—my cell phone battery went dead. There I sat, on the edge of a wintery country road, helpless. With all its bells and whistles, my phone was a paper weight and could not help me because it was not plugged in or charged up.

Paul's encouragement to Timothy to "continue" can be paraphrased as "stay plugged in" to the Word. The Word is our power source for the times when we feel stranded on the road of life. Too often we think we can run on our own batteries. Yes, maybe we can—for a while. But soon our spiritual battery runs dry as the struggles and pressures of life leave us feeling drained. Paul wasn't just expressing pious thoughts. He knew how important it was to "continue in what you have learned"—to *stay plugged in* to the Word. Use these devotions, and as many other opportunities as you have, to stay plugged in and connected to God's Word to keep your spiritual battery charged.

• How do you stay plugged in to the Word?

Pray: Lord, help me to stay connected to you throughout my life.

WEEK 40 DAY 2

Timothy Remembers His Teachers

❖

You know those from whom you learned it.
2 TIMOTHY 3:14

Context: 2 Timothy 3:14–17

Mr. Manthe, Mrs. Schommer, Mr. Paske, and Mr. Wilke may seem to be just names on a page, but to me they are more. They were my grade school teachers. They were the people who taught me math, science, and art; who disciplined me even if I did not feel I needed it; and who encouraged me daily in God's Word. Who was instrumental in teaching you about God? Was it your parents? your grandparents? your pastor? one or more teachers?

Timothy's father was Greek. Through his father, Timothy was probably introduced to Greek culture with its many gods and its thirst for wisdom as the key to all understanding. On the other side, he had his mother and grandmother, who made sure Timothy knew who the true God is and that Jesus is the Savior. Paul encouraged Timothy to remember those who taught him and to pay that forward as he went out and preached to others about Jesus.

As a teacher myself, this encouragement still sticks with me—to remember those who taught me. And the message they taught me, the gospel, motivates me to encourage the next generation—YOU! Our wisdom and culture have value, but they get us only so far. A relationship with Jesus will carry us all the way through the school of life, until we get to heaven where the recess is eternal.

- Take a moment to pray for or contact a teacher or mentor who has been influential in your faith.

Pray: Lord, thank you for those who taught me about Jesus. May I continue to follow their example as I teach others about you.

A Christian ID Equals Love

❖

"You have heard that it was said, 'Love your neighbor and hate your enemy.' But I tell you, love your enemies and pray for those who persecute you."

MATTHEW 5:43,44

Context: Matthew 5:43-48

If you have a driver's license, you probably remember your driver's test. First came the written test. If you managed to pass on your first try, you progressed to the behind-the-wheel test. Did you pass the first time? How many points were taken off?

As nerve-racking as the written and behind-the-wheel tests were, none of that prepared you for what came next—your ID photo. Oh man, you should have thought a little more about what to wear and how to have your hair. You would be showing your ID picture for years to come.

You couldn't help but be nervous as the person behind the camera told you where to stand and "to look natural." No matter how much you smiled—or tried—you do not like your ID picture. But you carry your driver's license with you wherever you go. You show it when you need to pick up a prescription at the pharmacy, when you need to get into certain places, or when an officer of the law pulls you over.

As Christians, we have ID cards too. What does yours look like? Jesus gives us a *picture* of what a Christian's ID card is to look like—*love!*

The love that he showed on the cross, modeled in his life of service, and poured on us at our baptisms is the image we reflect to those around us.

- What part does your Christian ID play in your relationship with your neighbor?

Pray: Lord, thank you for so clearly displaying your love in my life. May I be a picture of that love to everyone else.

A Christian ID—Lack of Vengeance

❖

"You have heard that it was said, 'Eye for eye, and tooth for tooth.' But I tell you, do not resist an evil person. If anyone slaps you on the right cheek, turn to them the other cheek also."
MATTHEW 5:38,39

Context: Matthew 5:38-42

Recently, my older brother and his family were in town. As our wives were busy shopping, he and I were busy babysitting. This consisted of watching a movie while the kids were napping. We watched the movie *Taken* starring Liam Neeson. After his daughter was "taken," we were entertained for 93 minutes as we watched Neeson take down the bad guys and let them know he has a particular set of skills.

How often don't we like to play that same revenge plotline out in our lives? Someone does something to me; I want to retaliate. Someone trash talks me; I need to get them back and trash their name. Someone pushes me on the court; I need to push them back. When we look in the mirror, or show our ID cards, we see that we are no better than the criminals Neeson was fighting in his movie.

Enter our action star Jesus, who has *taken* away our sins, even for the times we have disrespected our neighbor. He has *taken* the punishment we deserve, and he has *taken* God's anger, which rightfully should have been pointed toward us.

He has given us a new ID. This one is not tarnished with past mistakes but is covered in his blood. It says, *"You pass because I, Jesus, have taken away your sin!"*

- Why is it so hard to forgive?

Pray: Lord, thank you for taking away my sin!

121

WEEK 41 DAY 2

A Christian ID—Love for Neighbors

❖

"You have heard that it was said, 'Love your neighbor and hate your enemy.' But I tell you, love your enemies and pray for those who persecute you."
MATTHEW 5:43,44

Context: Matthew 5:43–48

Do you know who your neighbor is? Back in the day, neighbors would just get together for socializing. Sometimes they would walk to church together. But that has all changed.

Recently, my wife needed a Minion costume. (Long story for another sermon.) My former assistant coach had one. We just needed to pick it up at his home in the next town. I pulled up to the house I thought was his and walked to the door. After looking around, I wasn't sure I was at the right place, but I quietly knocked on the door. The person who answered the door was *not* my assistant coach or his wife. Startled, I asked the woman, "Do you know where Josh lives?" She responded, "I have never heard of that name before, and I have lived here for over 10 years." In the meantime, my wife had connected with my former coach. Can you guess where his house was? About 25 feet to the right. This lady didn't even recognize the name of her next-door neighbor.

Jesus shows the ultimate love and concern for everyone. As the nails were being pounded into his wrists for you, his prayer was not a prayer of vengeance. Instead, we get that clear ID photo of what true love looks like when we hear him say, "Father, forgive them." His forgiveness empowers us to do something that seems unnatural and is very difficult—to love even our enemies.

- What gets in the way of us showing love to others?

Pray: Lord, the greatest way we can show love to others is to share your name with them. Give me the courage to be that kind of good neighbor.

Jesus Deals With Grief

❖

"My soul is overwhelmed with sorrow."
MARK 14:34

Context: Mark 14:32–42

When people mourn a death, they generally go through five stages of grief: denial, anger, bargaining, depression, and resolution. Those who have felt the pain of death and have experienced that heartbreak or loss know these steps all too well. When my brother died in a snowmobile accident, I did not believe it had happened. I was waiting for him to come walking through the door. The moments after he died were surreal. When I realized he was not coming back, I blamed him for taking chances with his life. And I blamed God. I then played the mind tennis game: I should have done this, or I could have done that. Eventually, I realized that this was useless. Then the real depression set in, and I was in a dark place with Satan's claws sinking into my heart and mind. Thankfully, God gave me good friends. They may not have always had the words to say, but they were there and they listened to me. And I am not ashamed to admit that I went to a professional counselor who helped me get back on track.

I have now progressed to the resolution stage. The important thing is that my brother is in heaven. I know I could not have changed what happened. I also know this has made me empathetic toward others who experience this same type of loss. Perhaps you find yourself somewhere in the grief cycle. Do not be afraid to ask for help! If a friend is struggling with grief, reach out—and listen. Jesus endured overwhelming sorrow for us. With God's promise of eternal life in Jesus holding you up, you will be able to brave the storms.

- How might God use your troubles to help others?

Pray: Lord, you alone are my help, my strength, and my salvation.

Help From Hebrews

❖

**No discipline seems pleasant at the time, but painful.
Later on, however, it produces a harvest of righteousness
and peace for those who have been trained by it.**
HEBREWS 12:11

Context: Hebrews 12:7-12

After prayerful consideration about which of the two prep schools I should attend, my parents and I decided on the one located in Watertown. Though it was only ten minutes from my home, I lived in the dorms. My older brother teased that it was because my parents didn't love me. During my freshmen year, I cried myself to sleep every night because I was homesick.

I never understood why I had to deal with that pain for a whole year. For me, the answer came ten years later. I was called back to the same school to be a tutor (dorm supervisor and instructor). On the first day, I answered a knock on the door, and there stood a small, red-faced freshman with tears in his eyes. He immediately told me he was homesick. So after waiting ten years, I had an answer to my question about why I had to endure what I did. I helped Matt with his challenge the way my tutors had helped me ten years prior. We battled through it together with encouragement from Scripture.

Maybe you are struggling with an illness, a broken family, or challenging studies. Perhaps you too have asked, "Why, God?" The answer might be closer than you think. God may use these struggles to bring you closer to him or to prepare you so that you can help others who are going through something similar. Of one thing we can be sure: The Savior who loved us so much that he died for us still has our good in mind.

- Explain what this means: Man's extremity is God's opportunity.

Pray: During my times of struggle, help me to trust you and to learn from the experience so I can help others.

WEEK 42 DAY 2

Lost and Found

❖

"The Son of Man came to seek and to save the lost."
LUKE 19:10

Context: Luke 19:1-10

Some years ago I had to take a friend to Chicago's O'Hare Airport. As a new driver from the hill country of Farmington, I was unfamiliar with big city driving. While at the terminal, I got lost. Long story short: A construction worker pulled up and gave me directions. After thanking him, I again went the wrong way. How did I know? In my rearview mirror, I saw the construction worker flashing his truck lights. I slowed down. He pulled up alongside and said, "You are going the wrong way. FOLLOW ME."

Life is often described as a journey. We think we know where we are going, only to find out we are lost. We think we are in control of a situation but find we aren't. I won't be tempted to sin if I go to that party where everyone will be drinking. But I do go, and I do drink. I can be mature on our date. But I'm not, and we go too far.

We think we know more than our teachers or parents who give us directions and encourage us to take the right road for our lives.

God says to us, "You, my precious child, were lost. Now you are found." God, through his Son Jesus, has forgiven us for every time we have taken the wrong way. God is in front of us. He is behind us, flashing his lights and telling us, "FOLLOW ME." When we are lost, trust that God, who has gone to such great lengths to find us, knows the way. He's been to the future. Follow HIM!

• Compare the Bible to a GPS.

Pray: Lord, without you I am lost. Thank you for rescuing me.

Peter: Hero to Zero

❖

**Jesus . . . said to Peter, "Get behind me, Satan! . . .
You do not have in mind the concerns of God,
but merely human concerns."**
MATTHEW 16:23
Context: Matthew 16:21-27

A common plotline in movies depicts a good guy making it big, being dragged down by some creative form of adversity, and then coming out in the end as the victor.

Peter was a good guy, a disciple of Jesus. But he stuck his foot in his mouth when he tried to scold Jesus for talking about his impending suffering and death. Jesus really tore into Peter, and rightfully so.

Jesus understood Peter's problem: "You do not have in mind the concerns of God, but merely human concerns." Peter was very one dimensional in his thinking. He didn't see the big picture of what Jesus was talking about. Like Peter, we get so wrapped up in our own little world that we fail to realize the simple truths: God is still in control on good days and bad, and he has a plan to carry out in our lives.

Our moods and our lives may change, but GOD NEVER CHANGES! His love for us endures forever. What's more, he uses the so-called bad situations in our lives to bring us closer to him and his Word in order to strengthen our faith. And if that isn't enough, he forgives us for the times we doubt, stick our feet in our mouths, and do or say dumb things.

Rejoice! Because of Christ, your movie plot will always end well.

- Why is it hard to tell a friend that what they are doing is wrong?

- How might God be using some of your challenges today to prepare you for tomorrow?

Pray: Jesus, help me to focus on the things of God rather than on myself.

Hebrews—You Are Not Alone

❖

"Never will I leave you; never will I forsake you."
HEBREWS 13:5
Context: Hebrews 13:5,6

Once, when I was very small, my mom took me shopping so she could buy some clothes. Something caught my eye in the toy section, and I wandered off. I looked at one shiny object after another. But when I turned around, I couldn't find my mother. After walking the entire store, I went to the customer service desk and told the woman behind the counter, "My mom is missing." She got on the PA system and announced, "We have a lost little boy at the front of the store. Can his mother please pick him up?" I looked at her and corrected her very sternly: "Excuse me; I'm not lost. My mom is."

We can chuckle at that. But this is how we are in life. We grow up in the Word. We stay close to our heavenly Father. But then we get lured away by the toys of the world. We wander off and get lost. And maybe later we wonder why God left us. But God reminds us in our reading today, "Never will I leave you; never will I forsake you."

Strong words from the God who sought us out (not the other way around), the God who sent his Son to forgive us all of our sins—ALL OF THEM—and is with us always. When my mom and I were reunited, she took me in her arms and gave me a big hug. Our heavenly Father loves each and every one of us dearly. And even if we want to fight and push him away, he never stops holding us. He never stops loving us.

- How long is "never"? What does that say about the comfort we find in God's promise?

Pray: God, keep me focused more on you and less on the toys of the world.

Paul Gives Perspective

❖

**The message of the cross is foolishness
to those who are perishing,
but to us who are being saved
it is the power of God.**
1 CORINTHIANS 1:18

Context: 1 Corinthians 1:18-24

How quickly our perspective can change. What if I told you that you have won an all-expenses paid trip on a deluxe ocean liner? You are upgraded to first class where you will enjoy meals, parties, and rubbing elbows with celebrities. You will be living high on life. What would you say? Sign me up? How about if the name of that ocean liner was the *Titanic?* Would your perspective change?

Many travel through life thinking it is a big party. Certainly, life can be a joy. As Christians, we have no reason to walk around with a sour look on our faces, even though the devil wants us to think that we do. However, if someone is going down a path that is questionable, as a friend we want to warn that person of the danger of swimming in the deep water of their sin. We want to toss them the life vest of Christ to stay afloat in this world. So many people in our world think the message of the cross is foolishness. We know that it is the power of God that saves us.

Many perished the night the *Titanic* sank because the ship didn't have nearly enough wooden lifeboats to hold all the people on board.

On the *wooden cross* of Calvary, Jesus was able to hold the full weight of all our sins. This gives us a new perspective on life.

- How does the cross change your perspective on what is important in your life?

Pray: Jesus, give me the vision to live with a heavenly perspective.

Paul Pauses to Live

❖

To me, to live is Christ and to die is gain.

PHILIPPIANS 1:21

Context: Philippians 1:20-22

DVR has to be one of the best inventions of the past decades. It has helped avert many an argument. If the show is at a point of high drama when my wife asks me to do a simple chore, instead of getting caught between the decision either to miss the action or disappoint my wife, I can simply hit the pause button, do the task, come back, and pick up right where the show left off. Once I was watching a sporting event when a friend called and asked to be picked up at the airport. I hit the pause button, drove the hour to pick him up, dropped him off, and got back to the match right where I left off. Granted, by then I knew the final score, but I still wanted to watch the end of the match.

In a certain way, the life of a Christian is like having DVR. True, there will be moments when you will wish you could hit pause but can't. There will undoubtedly be some moments of high drama in your life. However, rejoice in the fact that you know how the show is going to end. You already know that Jesus won the victory and that, because of Jesus, you are victorious. You not only *know* but you *have* the happy ending! You can live life knowing this is one hundred percent true. (You are now free to *pause* and smile!)

- How does knowing that in Christ you have the victory influence the way you look at challenges in your life?

Pray: Jesus, help me to pause and reflect on the blessings you have given me. Give me the courage to live for you!

Paul Defines Love

❖

Love is patient, love is kind.
It does not envy, it does not boast,
it is not proud. Love never fails.

1 CORINTHIANS 13:4,8

Context: 1 Corinthians 13:1-13

If you've been to a few weddings, you've no doubt heard this text preached as the basis of a few sermons.

The love Paul is talking about here isn't the flippant type of love that rolls off our lips when we say, "Oh, I love your hair," or, "I love this song." That type of love is built on emotion, and when built on emotion, it's like a pair of shoes. It gets worn out, fades, goes out of style, or is even replaced—in short, it doesn't last.

The love that Paul is talking about isn't the plotline of a *Scooby-Doo* mystery. It's the deepest expression of real love, written in Christ's blood—so rich, so red, so flowing from a cross—for you. Yes, that is love—love that is built on a commitment that God made to you—and he keeps his word. It is a love that does not fade, a love that is everlasting, a love that keeps loving and forgiving us despite our sins, a love that linked the Corinthian congregation together and that links us together as well.

Christ's love lives in us and motivates us to use the gifts he's given us to work together as a family of believers. In many schools, athletes sit here, cool teachers sit there, trendy dressers sit here, and music people sit there. Christ's love makes us different. We all sit *together* at the foot of the cross, where Christ's love motivates us to be *one*.

- How do you define and show love?

Pray: Lord, thank you for showing me what true love is. Help me to model that kind of love.

WEEK 44 DAY 2

Peter and Suffering

❖

Rejoice . . . as you participate in the sufferings of Christ, so that you may be overjoyed when his glory is revealed.
1 PETER 4:13

Context: 1 Peter 4:12-16

Being a fan of a team only when they are winning can result in only so much joy. But when you follow a team through its hard times and losing seasons, it becomes particularly sweet when they start winning! Today we focus on the trials that you experience *because* you are a Christian. Those trials come in many varied forms: persecution for your beliefs. The burden of sacrificing for and loving others, putting their needs before your own. The reality that you are going to follow training rules, no matter how hard, because you made a promise to your teammates and coaches and you know that is what God wants you to do. The challenge of loving that friend, no matter how difficult he or she makes it, because you love others as Jesus does.

If living this way causes inconvenience or suffering, don't be ashamed! Praise God for giving you the honor of honoring him with your life!

After a particularly embarrassing loss, the team's head coach showed class by not pointing fingers. Instead, he simply stated that there are no guarantees in football. How true. It's equally true that there are few guarantees in life. But no matter what kind of challenges you face, you do have one for sure guarantee: You're not alone. You have plenty of teammates alongside you, cheering you on. And you have the greatest coach of all, Jesus, motivating you with the promise that he has forgiven you and that with him you will always be a winner.

• What makes suffering beneficial?

Pray: Lord, whether I seem to be winning or losing, teach me to focus on you alone.

Love, Not Lust

❖

"I have loved you with an everlasting love."
JEREMIAH 31:3

Context: Jeremiah 31:3-9

A student once asked me when it's the right time to tell someone, "I love you." My answer: "When you are in a committed married relationship. I told many girls in my dating career that I loved them. Where are they now? Married to my best friends (and very happy to be with someone else)."

This brought laughs to the classroom. But it is true.

The Bible defines love in three ways: *eros*—the erotic love; *phileo*—the brotherly friendship kind of love; and *agape*—the ultimate, selfless, unconditional love. The first two forms of love have their place in a dating relationship. There is an attraction to someone you date. You also want to be with someone who shares common interests with you as a friend. But troubles arise when those first two kinds of love are the basis for a relationship and when God and the selfless heart are pushed into the background. Until there is that commitment to love the person who sometimes is unlovable, it is not true love.

God loves us even though we are unlovable, to the point that he died for us. That is exactly the kind of love he asks us to have for others, especially in our relationships. If we try to build our relationships without God or without reflecting his love, it's like playing in a three-on-three tournament with only two players. You are outmanned and outmuscled. When the best player in a relationship is missing, many couples try to compensate by focusing on the physical love and thus play into the devil's game. Christ modeled for you what true love is; he died for you and forgives all your sins. Pattern your relationship after his love.

- Think of times you have been the recipient of *agape* love from family members or friends.

Pray: Jesus, help me to pattern my life after your love.

God Freezes Fears, Part 1

❖

**God is our refuge and strength,
an ever-present help in trouble.**
PSALM 46:1

Context: Psalm 46:1–3

My favorite game in grade school was freeze tag. At the middle of one side of our gym, we had a wooden structure that game statisticians sat on during games. During recess, this served as "goal." What's goal? Goal was the one place you were safe. As long as you had your hand on goal, no one could tag you. Nothing could get at you or hurt you!

Those games were fun. But then we grew up, and now we have to play the game of life. We have stress at work, trouble at home, and drama with our friends at school. Real life threatens to overpower our spiritual lives. Our problems grab our attention, and we let them drown out our God's voice.

The psalmist reminds us that God is our goal—we are safe with him.

Psalm 46 was the basis for Luther's famous hymn "A Mighty Fortress Is Our God."

From the psalm's opening verses, God is described as our "refuge." In the original language, *refuge* means "shelter" or "protection from danger or distress." The main thought underlying the Hebrew term that is translated as "refuge" is security. Wait, there is more. God is also our "strength" and "an ever-present help in trouble."

If you go to the drugstore when you have a cold, do you want the normal cold relief or the extra strength? Of course, if you are miserable, you want the extra strength because it's stronger. When picking teams, whom do you pick to be on your team? The strongest—mentally and physically—because they will give you the best chance of victory. Our God is extra strength!

- When is it especially important for you to remember that God is your refuge?

Pray: Lord, thank you for being my refuge and strength.

WEEK 45 DAY 2

God Freezes Fears, Part 2

❖

**God is our refuge and strength,
an ever-present help in trouble.**
PSALM 46:1
Context: Psalm 46:1,8–11

Not too long ago I was at the local Barnes and Noble looking at the overpriced DVDs that my updated family budget says I'm not allowed to buy. As I was looking for the restroom, I had to chuckle. Those who say God doesn't have a sense of humor will appreciate this: tucked back by the restroom is the section labeled "Self-Help."

Now that's true to life. So often we get ourselves into messes and think that WE can help ourselves out of them. Usually we find out that the more we try to fix things, the worse it gets.

Fortunately for us, we have a God who is ALWAYS with us—24/7. He is a God who can walk on water, a God who can raise the dead, a God who can feed thousands with a young boy's lunch, a God who can defeat armies. This same God is your "refuge," your "strength." And not just when you feel it. He is an "ever-present help." Trust him. You are safe in his arms!

What is more, the devil and this sinful world no longer have power over us because our God, our strong refuge, defeated the devil on Calvary. Our sins are now washed clean in his blood. We are SAFE!!!

- Why is self-help really an oxymoron?

- Why is it a mistake to think that we can help ourselves out of a jam?

Pray: Lord, give me the confidence to know that you are always with me and that my help alone comes from you.

Chill Out

❖

"Be still, and know that I am God."
PSALM 46:10

Context: Psalm 46:10,11

Ever open the paper or watch the news and find yourself stunned to the point that you can't help asking, "What in the world is going on? Judgment day has to be around the corner."

In the verses preceding our reading, the psalmist indicates that the world of his day was also in chaos. "Nations are in uproar," he wrote in verse 6. Things were spinning out of control, yet he could say, "Be still, and know that I am God." Today, even if the world is falling apart around us, we can *be still* because our God is still in control.

Translating *be still* in the language of today, we might say *chill out*. Chill out, and know that God is in control.

Our problem is that though Jesus is in the driver's seat, we want to drive the car. With Jesus in the driver's seat, we can put our sins and our struggles in the rearview and just enjoy the ride. But we miss too much of life because we want to play God or we want to be driving. How much better for us if we just chill out and let God be God.

He reminds us in his Word over and over again that we have no need to worry and that we are safe. He says that you can chill out because "in all things God works for the good of those who love him" (Romans 8:28).

We have a God who invites us to lean on him, no matter how stressful our lives might be. Be still, and know that he is God.

- When your stress level is high, what can you do to "chill out"?

Pray: Lord, teach me to be still, to chill out and know that no matter what comes my way, you are GOD and you will work all things for my good.

135

Stephen Speaks BOLDLY

❖

Then the high priest asked Stephen, "Are these charges true?"
To this he replied: "Brothers and fathers, listen to me!"
ACTS 7:1,2

Context: Acts 7:1-60

You're sitting in the chair getting your hair cut and the conversation turns to your weekend plans. There's a hesitation, a pause, and you feel reluctant to say that you are going to church for fear the others might think you are weird. The answer "nothing much" seems to flow from our lips so easily.

A teenager struggles with the choice of doing what is right versus potentially losing friends, so he quietly picks up a beer at the party and starts drinking.

Or we can all relate to this one: We remain silent as a classmate or coworker is being cut down by others, saying nothing to defend the person's good name.

We've all been in situations where we have had opportunities to demonstrate or witness to our faith only to clam up and say nothing for fear of failure or rejection. Stephen, on the other hand, gives us an example of boldness.

Stephen was simply following the example of the apostles who stood before the Sanhedrin and boldly spoke these words: "We must obey God rather than human beings!" (Acts 5:29).

The easy way out for Stephen would have been to keep his mouth shut. But Stephen was not there to win a popularity contest. Instead, he realized that what was more important—the one thing needful—was his relationship with God.

Though we may not want to lose friends, we realize that our salvation (and theirs) does not rest on what others think of us but rather on what Jesus has done for us. Trust him! Do not be afraid! You are not alone!

- In what areas do you wish you could be more bold?

Pray: Lord, give me the strength to be a bold witness for you.

Two Unalike But Equally Saved

❖

There was a Pharisee, a man named Nicodemus. JOHN 3:1
A Samaritan woman came to draw water. JOHN 4:7
Context: John 3:1-16; 4:4-26,39-41

I played sports, but I wasn't a star player. I enjoyed music, but I never had the leading role in a musical. And I got average grades. But I was friends with those who were the stars of the court, the stage, and the classroom.

Your teen years can be rough because you tend to measure your status by your accomplishments.

The simple truth is that we all fall short of what we would need to be in order to have a relationship with God. We all deserve death. This applies also to the person who makes the heroic play that wins the game, the person who performs the lead on stage, and the person who always has the right answer in class.

It is also true that God died to save everyone, no matter your race, class, or gender—or whether or not you wear brand-name clothes.

Our context readings above show us Jesus as he taught a valuable lesson to two people who were very much on opposite ends of society's social spectrum. Nicodemus belonged to the elite group of his day, the Jewish ruling council, but his elite status didn't save him. It was his relationship with Jesus that did. The same goes for the Samaritan woman, who was the outcast in her town. Her conversation with Jesus brought her to know her Savior. More than that, Jesus used this woman to be a great missionary in her town to save even more souls. That too is a testament to our God's amazing grace. Share that grace today with someone who needs it, no matter who they are or what they look like!

- Call, text, and/or email someone who needs encouragement.

Pray: Lord, help me to see me how you see me: as loved.

Influenced by Jesus

❖

**Nicodemus, who had gone to Jesus earlier and
who was one of their own number, asked,
"Does our law condemn a man without first hearing him
to find out what he has been doing?"**
JOHN 7:50,51
Context: John 7:45-52

What is the first memory you have of hearing about Jesus? Was it perhaps as a family member was singing, "Jesus loves me, this I know"?

Over the course of our lives, God has used many different people to influence the growth of our faith. Now you are getting to the age where you recognize the impact you can have on the lives of others, especially those who are younger than you.

Christ's servant attitude is both our model and our motivation.

Jesus delighted in teaching and preaching to everyone and anyone. He loved all equally—the rich and the poor, the timid and the bold. He also knew that there was one thing that was needful for all. So he patiently taught Nicodemus. And look at the impact. Nicodemus, who came to Jesus at night so that no one would see him, had the courage to stand up for him in front of the entire ruling council and later to ask for Jesus' body so he could bury him in a respectful tomb. Most important of all, he knew that Jesus was his Savior.

The world influences us in negative ways. It is easy to become *me centric*. Sadly, I have sometimes allowed myself to be influenced negatively, and I have not always been the best influence on others. But I keep coming back to the simple truth that I learned long ago: "Jesus loves me, this I know." Sometimes being an influence on others begins in very simple ways.

- What mentor has impacted your life? Does he or she know this? Think of others you can influence in a positive way.

Pray: Lord, help me to be a positive influence on others—through and for you.

Jesus Prays

❖

He went up on a mountainside by himself to pray.
MATTHEW 14:23
Context: Matthew 14:13-23

What is your morning routine? Hit the snooze eight times, roll out of bed, and throw some makeup on? Or a shower followed by a hearty breakfast and a quick check of Twitter before you head to work or school?

Routines can provide comfort or help us tackle situations staring us in the face. But we have something more valuable than grooming or our morning cup of joe to get us through the day. We have the gift of prayer.

Jesus had just fed more than five thousand people and soon would show his power over gravity by walking on the water. Between these two momentous displays of his glory, what did he do? Take a power nap or sign autographs? No, he took time out of his day to pray—to bring the needs of the people to his heavenly Father.

Where does prayer fit in our daily routine?

Prayer is important; it is our direct connection to God. And it is always available.

Sometimes we may feel that we have been praying to God but that he doesn't answer. Perhaps God doesn't answer right away because he wants us to keep talking to him. If he immediately gave us everything we asked for, our conversations would end up being very short and probably very focused on ourselves. So if God doesn't answer immediately, think about it like this: maybe he's saying, "Keep talking. Keep asking. I am listening." Or perhaps, "I have already answered your request, but you didn't hear me." Or, "I have something better in mind." Whatever your prayer, whatever your routine, know that God is listening to you *completely!*

- What helps you get into the routine of prayer?

Pray: Lord, teach me to pray and to trust your answer.

Peter Looks and Leaps

❖

Peter got down out of the boat, walked on the water and came toward Jesus.
MATTHEW 14:29

Context: Matthew 14:22-32

Once, while on a trip to the remote island of Antigua, I cliff jumped. It's simple: you walk to the top of a three-story cliff and jump into the ocean below. It's an amazing feeling. You jump, having faith that everything will be okay when your body hits the water.

That first step out of the boat for Peter must have been a doozy. You can imagine what was going through his mind: *You have fished these waters for years. You know that it isn't physically possible to stand on it.* Yet, Jesus was right in front of him, walking on the water. So Peter's first step was okay. But when he took his eyes off of Jesus and looked at the wave hurtling his way, he was sunk.

What difficult decision are you facing? "Where should I go to college? What job should I take? Should I have the courage to stand up to my friends when they are clearly living lifestyles that aren't right?"

When we face struggles and temptations and are confronted with decisions we have to make in life, all too often we take our eyes off of Jesus. Fortunately, we have a Savior who never takes his eyes off of us.

While we may not see him physically, he is with us always. Whenever we open the pages of Scripture, he speaks to us, saying, "Do not be afraid." A Savior who can lift the load of sin from our shoulders certainly can take care of us even when challenging waves threaten to wash over us. Don't focus on your problems; focus on Jesus.

- What leap of faith do you need to take today?

Pray: Lord, help me to trust you even when I struggle with doubt.

Peter Gives Us Casting Lessons

❖

Cast all your anxiety on him because he cares for you.
1 PETER 5:7

Context: 1 Peter 5:6,7

My first attempt at fishing was memorable. I got the hook stuck in my thumb, my brother's leg, my father's cap, a piece of wood, and a boat cushion. Eventually I learned some lessons, and casting actually became fun. We even had competitions, not about catching the most fish but about who could cast the farthest. There is a certain satisfaction you get in just letting that line go and watching it float across the water.

Peter tells us that when life gives us problems, we can cast them on God! Our problem is that when we are stressed and worried, we want to reel them back in and carry them around.

Imagine that you get dressed for work or school. But before leaving your residence, you are handed a 45-pound weight and are told to put it in your backpack, jacket, or briefcase and to carry it around with you all day. What would your reaction be? "No way am I carrying that extra weight around all day; it would be silly." Then why do we insist on carrying around the weight of life that weighs us down? That too is silly. Cast it on God! His hands can carry all of your problems. Those same hands took the full weight of the world's sins when he was lifted on a cross. So he can handle it. Is it time to start casting your problems away?

• Why is it hard to let go of stress and to let God handle it?

Pray: Lord, right now I am casting all my cares on you. Give me courage to trust that you alone can carry them so that I don't keep reeling them back in.

Peter Makes Us Aware of Our Enemy

❖

**Be alert and of sober mind.
Your enemy the devil prowls
around like a roaring lion looking
for someone to devour.**
1 PETER 5:8

Context: 1 Peter 5:8-11

What is your biggest fear? Like Indiana Jones, I hate snakes. I am not a fan of spiders either. (I am the manly man who uses 52 paper towels to kill one spider.) And I am definitely not a fan of lions. Yes, even *The Lion King* movie has to be viewed with all the lights on in our home.

The lion is one of the fiercest animals. It shouldn't surprise us that the devil is compared to a roaring lion. The devil is a predator—he knows when and how to attack us. He will pounce when we are at our weakest. Are you stressed over work, a home situation, what's happening at school, or your relationships? The devil will play the mind tennis game to get you to doubt God: "Come on, does God really love you? If he did, he would not let this happen to you." When you find yourself in the jungle (and everyone faces those moments), don't imagine that you can stand up and face this lion alone. Run to God for safety. If you aren't feeling close to God, remember, God hasn't moved. God went into the ring with the devil and defeated the lion. The lion has been declawed. He is caged. Caged lions can't get you unless you get too close. Resist him, and he will flee from you.

- What else can the devil be compared to?

- How can you prepare for the devil's attacks?

Pray: Lord, help me recognize the devil as he crouches in the weeds getting ready to attack, and help me flee his attacks.

Peter—Not Alone

❖

**You know that the family of believers
throughout the world
is undergoing the same kind of sufferings.**
1 PETER 5:9

Context: 1 Peter 5:9-11

My teenage brother took me to the local fair once. Or, more appropriately, my parents forced him to take me. He quickly became bored watching me ride the kiddie rides, so he asked me a question I will never forget: "Do you want to go into the haunted house?" What six-year-old wouldn't want to go? But, of course, he sent me in alone. *(TV timeout) In Sunday school that week, our teacher had told us that whenever we are nervous, we should just start singing. (Back to the action)* So picture little six-year-old me walking into this haunted house. As soon as I stepped on the contraption that made the witch, mummy, and Dracula light up, I crouched down into a fighting stance and began to sing "A Mighty Fortress Is Our God" at the top of my lungs. I bet it was rather amusing to others. But I made it through because I knew I was not alone.

Life may seem like a ride. Sometimes it can be scary—or downright frightening. In our reading, Peter reminds us of two important truths: (1) The problems we face only last a little while. (2) We are not alone. We have a God who is always with us, and we have a family of believers that we can rely on. Yes, that is something to sing about—with joy in our hearts!

Cue the music now!

- What is your favorite hymn? Under what kinds of situations might you sing that hymn for your own comfort?

Pray: Lord, help me to see that I am not alone on this ride called life.

A Humble Heart

❖

Humble yourselves before the Lord, and he will lift you up.

JAMES 4:10

Context: James 4:7-10

This past summer, I actually read a few books—yes, books with big words and hardly any pictures. (I know; we all have to grow up sometime.) One book that I particularly liked was about the life and career of the famous UCLA coach John Wooden. In this book, many of Coach Wooden's former players discussed his team philosophy, which made him a person they wanted to follow and play for. He expressed his philosophy in many different ways, but three key points stood out: (1) "Success is about doing the little things." Players talked about how, in their first practice, they didn't run any plays. Instead, they would watch as this older gentleman demonstrated how to properly wear a pair of socks and how to properly tie their shoes. (2) "Selfless teamwork is great teamwork." He emphasized that when you are part of a team, you are not in it for yourself. And (3) "There is power in humility." Many of the players mentioned the importance of this belief.

Today a different author, James, encourages us with the reminder that God exalts the humble. Yes, Coach Wooden was a great coach. Some would say that he will go down in history as *the* greatest. However, the one who was put on the *wooden cross* will always be the greatest. *His story, his humility,* and *his love* for others—*for you*— accomplished something no one else ever could. And it inspires love and dedication that no one else could inspire. We live our lives for him, but with humility, because he did it all.

- What life lessons have coaches or teachers taught you that you can apply to your spiritual life?

Pray: Lord, teach me to focus on the little things in order to show your great love to others.

God Calls Matthew

❖

He saw a man named Matthew sitting at the tax collector's booth. "Follow me," he told him.
MATTHEW 9:9

Context: Matthew 9:9-13

During my junior year of high school, I was removed from the football team for breaking training rules. I messed up. As a result of my stupidity, some looked at me like I was from another planet. Though most people treated me like a leper, one teacher pulled me aside and reminded me not to let my past define who I was. He stated that my true character would be shown by how I would go on from there. Those words have always stuck with me.

Matthew had a sketchy past. He worked for the enemy. And if he was the typical tax collector of his day, he stole from his friends. Racked with guilt, Matthew may well have had issues sleeping at night. But then it happened. God called him. Yes, Matthew, this thieving enemy of the nation, was given a second chance. He did not let his past define him. Instead, his relationship with his Savior defined who he was. Now when people think of Matthew, they think of the disciple who was forgiven and now has his name at the top of the list of the books of the New Testament.

As you read this, perhaps you are racked with guilt over a past sin. Friends, do not let that define you. Instead, listen to the Savior's voice as he invites you to follow him to the cross where you will find forgiveness for all of your sins. *All of them!*

Now what is your next move? If God can use Matthew and this sinful author, he certainly can and will use you!

- Imagine that your pastor asks you to teach VBS. If you feel unqualified, what does this lesson say to you?

Pray: Lord, remind me that what counts is how you see me. Let your love always define who I am.

All Are Welcome at Matthew's Table

❖

While Jesus was having dinner at Matthew's house, many tax collectors and sinners came and ate with him.
MATTHEW 9:10

Context: Matthew 9:9-13

I love Jesus! Yes, for the obvious reasons of his death and his resurrection but also because he did not pick favorites.

Growing up can be difficult. God may not have gifted you in some areas, and you may wonder why not. Why can't I make the winning basket in the game or even get some minutes on the floor? Why can't I have the nice clothes or sit at the table with the popular kids?

Matthew was not Mr. Popular. In fact, you might have called him Mr. Hated. Hated by his own people for stealing from them. Hated because he worked for the enemy. That Matthew was shunned by others didn't stop Jesus from picking him to be one of his own disciples. In response, Matthew threw a party to which he invited fellow sinners. Seated around the table were those no one else wanted anything to do with—sinners. But among them was also our Savior, who came to die for them—and for you and me.

Okay, what does this have to do with you? (1) No matter what gift you think you have or do not have, Jesus loves you and wants to dine with you. He does not exclude you from his dinner party. (2) If you are someone who has been given gifts, look out for those who do feel shunned. Be like Matthew: Invite them to your table or to dine with you. And don't just follow the example of Jesus; also introduce them to Jesus. He is their best friend too!

- How do you define self-righteous? Why is a self-righteous attitude so destructive?

Pray: Jesus, teach me to follow you and to treat all people the way you treat me.

Fishers of People

❖

**"Come, follow me," Jesus said, "and I will send you
out to fish for people."**
MATTHEW 4:19

Context: Matthew 4:18-22

Do you love to hunt or fish? Neither of these hobbies is my first choice. But before you chuck this book into the garbage, please let me explain. I do like to hunt and fish. What I do NOT care for is all the time and patience these hobbies require in order to be successful. Getting up in the wee hours of the morning in the cold or sitting out in the boat for what seems like days can really try one's patience. I prefer my bed to the deer stand or boat.

Sharing your faith is much the same. When you share your faith, it takes patience and persistence. Just because you asked a friend to come to church once and they made an excuse doesn't mean you give up. You keep asking. Or you find a different way to ask them. Fishers or hunters who catch or see nothing don't give up. Instead, they go right back at it the next day or perhaps just find a different spot. We too practice patience in interacting with those with whom we share the gospel.

More important, we remember that we are not the ones attracting these people to Christ. It is the Holy Spirit. The fisher uses bait to catch the fish, and we use the gospel as our net to catch souls for Christ. Do not be afraid; you are not alone. Start casting now!

- If you feel unqualified, read Acts 4:13 to see what type of people Jesus chose for this fishing mission.

Pray: Lord, teach me to be patient and persistent when it comes to sharing your name.

Fathers Versus the Heavenly Father

❖

As a father has compassion on his children, so the LORD
has compassion on those who fear him.
PSALM 103:13

Context: Psalm 103:1-6,13,14

How do you picture God? When God is compared to a father, do positive or negative thoughts come to mind? For many of us, our fathers were the source of discipline. I can remember a few well-deserved spankings. And yet, because we know how loving and caring our fathers are, most of us have very positive feelings that we associate with our earthly fathers. However, the word *earthly* points to at least one negative. Our fathers are sinful. Perhaps you are marked with pain because of a father who hurt you, a father who abandoned you, or a father whose harsh lifestyle made you grow up faster than you wanted.

As we grow up, we may tend to pass our earthly associations of a father on to our heavenly Father. As much as I love my family, I'll admit that we were a *yell first, ask questions later* type of family. As a result, that's how I picture God at times. Do you? God is NOT going to abandon you! He is not waiting for you to mess up. When you mess up, Satan will try to tell you to distance yourself from God because God could never forgive you. FALSE! When we mess up, God wants us to run to him! He punished Jesus in our place and wants you to know that he will never leave you. As a father myself, I know I am not perfect. Only Jesus is. My own weaknesses have made me more empathetic to my parents and more thankful to my heavenly Father for never letting me down.

- What other thoughts influence the way you picture God?

Pray: Heavenly Father, thank you for always loving me and being there for me, even when I do not realize it.

Father's Hands

❖

**"My Father . . . is greater than all; no one can snatch
them out of my Father's hand."**
JOHN 10:29
Context: John 10:27-30

We do everything we can to protect our identities. Credit cards now have embedded chips as another layer of protection. In order to update a setting on my iTunes account, I had to receive a verification code on another device and enter that code into the computer. Yet, with all that protection, the hackers still seem to get through.

Spiritually, we also have a double layer of protection—an even greater one. Out of love, God sent his Son to die for you. He raised Jesus to give you eternal life. Jesus has invested his life in you. And he says about his Father's children, "No one can snatch them out of my Father's hand."

Sometimes we aren't so sure. Like the young boy who is told to leap into his father's arms from the second-floor window of his burning home, as the smoke clouds his eyes, he screams, "Daddy, I can't see you." To which his father replies, "You can't see me, but I can see you."

"God is our refuge and strength, an ever-present help in trouble" (Psalm 46:1). *He sees you!* When you walk through the valley of the shadow of death, you have the Savior-Shepherd to protect you. When you breathe your last breath, the arms that were outstretched on Calvary's cross will be there to welcome you home. So as we go through life, we may have doubts. Whenever we do, we can look to the cross to see how much we are loved. We can look in the mirror and see God's prized creation.

- How can we be a mirror to others to let them know they too are protected?

Pray: Lord, teach me to believe that even when I do not see you, you always see me and know what is best.

Mathletes

❖

**Do not add to what I command you and
do not subtract from it,
but keep the commands of the LORD your God
that I give you.**

DEUTERONOMY 4:2

Context: Deuteronomy 4:1,2

Even though I was a D+ student in math, I have to admit that math is something we all need in life. After taking your significant other out for a nice dinner, you need to leave a tip. How much do you leave: 10, 15, or 20 percent? Or if you're single and want to get the waiter's or waitress's phone number, perhaps you overtip. But how much is that? Boom! You need math.

Math, however, is not good when it comes to the Word!

Present-day Pharisees may make up or add rules or laws to what God has said in his Word. Some have decided that their own opinions are more important than God's standards. We are also tempted to play the subtraction game. We will say, "Yes, God loves me and forgives me because I deserve it," conveniently leaving out what God says about our sinful natures. Or we'll subtract "as yourself" from the "you shall love your neighbor as yourself" equation and we'll hold grudges or trash our neighbors rather than build them up.

God would have every right to hit the delete button and be done with us. Instead, he put Jesus into the equation. None of us are able to solve this equation for x: $x = $ *how to get to heaven on your own*. The math just doesn't add up. But Jesus is the solution.

So do the math, and see that God alone has made us *whole*. No way would we want to add to or subtract from his Word.

- Where did the Pharisees go wrong in their pursuit of keeping the law? Why are we tempted to do the same?

Pray: Jesus, thank you for taking 3 nails and 1 cross, making me 4-given!

Objects in the Mirror

❖

**What other nation is so great as to have their gods near them
the way the LORD our God is near us whenever we pray to him?**
DEUTERONOMY 4:7

Context: Deuteronomy 4:7,8

Do we think of God the way we think of a vehicle that we see
in our car's side mirror? He's there, but just how close? On dates,
God can't be there when we're alone and the lights are off, can he?
Or in class, when the teacher isn't watching? I mean, I don't see
him in my mirrors.

When we look into the mirror of God's law, we see how often
we have been reckless drivers with his Word.

Perhaps you don't feel close to God anymore. You're not the
grade school hero you once were—maybe you even get cut from
the team. The friends who say they'll always be there for you are
jumping out of your vehicle left and right and hitching rides with
"cooler" friends. And when you hit the bumpy roads, you start
looking in the mirror, asking, "Okay, where are you, God? Are
you even there?" The psalmist reminds us, "The LORD is near
to all who call on him, to all who call on him in truth" (Psalm
145:18). Moses spoke the words above to the nation of Israel as
he was preparing them for the day he would no longer be around
to guide them. He wanted them to remember that God was near
them. That reminder is our comfort as well. God is near us.

We are children whom Jesus valued so much that he was willing
to die for us. Even if we can't see God, HE IS CLOSE TO EACH
ONE OF US.

- When do you fail to see God? How can you sharpen your
  vision so that you do see him?

Pray: Lord, teach me to "be still, and know that [you are] God"
(Psalm 46:10).

Wise Guys

❖

**Observe them carefully, for this will show your wisdom
and understanding to the nations, who will hear about
all these decrees and say, "Surely this great nation is a wise
and understanding people."**
DEUTERONOMY 4:6

Context: Deuteronomy 4:5,6

While I was watching TV, my mom came into the room and said, "Clark, don't sit so close or your eyes will get crossed." Without missing a beat, I turned to her, purposely crossed my eyes, and said, "What mother? I have no idea what you are talking about." And yes, I did say it with a British accent. And yes, my mom did smack me on the head as she said, "Don't be such a wise guy!"

Have you ever been called a wise guy?

Moses reminded the Israelites that their success in battle was not a product of their military strength. In a similar way, our security and success won't be found in bank accounts or in popularity. In both cases, what is needed is the true wisdom that is found in one place alone: the Holy Scriptures. "The Holy Scriptures . . . are able to make you wise for salvation through faith in Christ Jesus" (2 Timothy 3:15).

The voice of our reason often mimics the voice of the devil, saying, "You don't need God." Or, "You know everything you need to know from the Bible. You don't need to pay attention to or stay anchored in the Word. You don't need to go to church."

Israel's history shows clearly that when they distanced themselves from God, things did not go well. When they were close to God, God kept them close to him. We will have challenges in life. But we will also have wisdom from God's Word—wisdom that brings peace.

- What steps can you take to become wise by God's standards?

Pray: Lord, help me to continue to be wise in you.

Centurion's Faith

❖

"Just say the word, and my servant will be healed."
MATTHEW 8:8

Context: Matthew 8:5-10

I remember watching as my brother stood on the platform while a voice counted down from ten. When the voice said, "One!" my brother leaped into the open air. As we watched him free fall several stories, our hearts raced. Then the elastic rope did what it's supposed to do; it stretched and began to bounce as my brother's screams turned to laughter. He had bungee jumped. I remember asking him afterwards if he had been scared. He said, "Nope. I trusted that everything was going to do what it does."

Maybe you have shown that kind of blind trust too. When you have a headache, you go to the cabinet and take two aspirins, trusting that they will help. Or you get into your car (most cars) and turn the key, trusting that the complex electrical system under the hood is going to do what it does. We trust without thinking about it.

This sums up the faith of the centurion. He trusted Jesus' power. He knew that Jesus did not have to be present physically to heal his servant. He trusted that Jesus' words alone could do that.

God's Word is powerful. Jesus' words alone calmed the storm. Jesus' words alone told a dead friend to come out of his grave. Jesus' words alone are what give us comfort when we feel the pressures of life weighing down on us. While bungee jumping might not be on the top of your list of things to do, might I suggest jumping into the pages of Scripture for thrills?

• What prevents you from having a centurion-like faith?

Pray: Lord, give me a faith like the centurion, which completely trusts your Word.

Faith Floats

❖

**When Jesus heard this, he was amazed and said
to those following him, "Truly I tell you, I have not found
anyone in Israel with such great faith."**
MATTHEW 8:10

Context: Matthew 8:10-13

A teacher once compared faith to a life preserver. You could have one finger on the life preserver and it will still keep you above water. He went on to say that you could have both hands wrapped tightly around it and it will still do what it does—FLOAT.

Our faith is our grip, and the life preserver, JESUS, keeps us afloat. We can have one or both hands on the precious truths of the Word and we will be saved. "Then why does it matter if I go to church or stay in the Word if I can get by with just one finger on the Bible?" The teacher anticipated the question. He grabbed a Bible and said, "This is the life preserver. Now imagine that a big wave of doubt or depression comes your way—what happens then?" At this point he asked one of the students to pull the life preserver out of his one hand. The student did so with ease. "It's easy for the storms of life to knock you off of the life preserver."

He then grabbed onto the Bible with both hands and said, "Imagine all of life's problems come tumbling down on you like a wave. You will survive the wave attack because your life preserver keeps you afloat."

Because you are in the Word, you keep your eyes on the life preserver. The Holy Spirit works in your heart to make you strong. Jesus is our life preserver; he alone keeps us afloat when life hands us waves. Hold on tightly to him!

- What are ways we can tighten our grip on our life preserver?

Pray: Jesus, please help me to have a tight grip on you when the waves of life come crashing down.

WEEK 52 DAY 2

Last Call

❖

**When hard pressed, I cried to the LORD;
he brought me into a spacious place.
The LORD is with me; I will not be afraid.
What can mere mortals do to me?**
PSALM 118:5,6

Context: Psalm 118:5-9

I am not good with goodbyes. I will either drag them out or I just flat out race through the words and hang up before the other person can respond. This is not meant to be rude; it's just that I do not want the moment to end.

Scholars say that Psalm 118 may have been one of the last Passover songs Jesus sang with his disciples in the upper room. How fitting to close out his earthly life with such a beautiful picture. He knew what was coming, but still he pressed on.

It is this picture that I want to leave you with. We have gone on this journey together. And you will continue your journey after this book has been put down. My prayer is that when you feel the pressures of life, you will remember where to turn, you will remember the spacious place provided by the promises of God. Turn to the Lord! When the world seems against you, remember that you do not need to be afraid because our awesome God is more powerful than anyone or anything in this world.

The refrain of an older song says, "Every new beginning comes from some other beginning's end" ("Closing Time" by Semisonic). Christ's walk to the cross was the end of his earthly life, but it was the beginning of our eternal life with him. Say goodbye to the rule of sin and Satan and hello to our new beginnings in Christ.

- Where is your spacious place to go when you are hard-pressed?

Pray: Lord, thank you for always being with me. With you, I have no reason to be afraid.

155

Easter Egg Devotion

❖

**The creation waits in eager expectation
for the children of God to be revealed.**
ROMANS 8:19
Context: Romans 8:18,19,31-37

The movie ends. You are in awe. You turn to your friend and say, "That was amazing!" The director and actors took you on a journey that left you breathless. As the closing credits begin to roll, you are about to exit the theater, when BOOM, the theater goes dark and there on the screen is a one-minute snippet of a scene from an upcoming movie. Marvel Comics has made this their go-to tactic. This "Easter egg," as they call it, gives a sneak preview of what is to come. So you leave the theater even more eager, counting the days until the short scene you just saw will play out as a full-length movie.

Life plays out similarly. There were days this past year that left us shaking our heads in amazement! There were also those dark theater days that we would prefer to fast-forward through. The good days we have are just a fraction—an Easter egg—of the happiness that will be revealed when we get to live the full movie FOREVER in heaven. The first Easter, the empty tomb, guarantees that something better is coming. Rejoice! You are a child of God.

As we close this book, remember, life is a journey. Do not stress about where you are headed—the preview God has given us in the Bible is already a reality in Christ! Instead, focus on who is leading and who is always with you!

- How can a Christian be eager and patient at the
  same time?

Pray: My risen Easter King, thank you for sticking with me through the good and the bad this past year. Help me eagerly look forward to your return.